WELCOME TO ROTA:

The Unofficial Guide to Getting Settled and
Enjoying the Culture, Food, and Travel
Opportunities of Southern Spain

LIZANN LIGHTFOOT

ISBN: 1497437644
ISBN-13: 978-1497437647

DEDICATION

This book is dedicated to my husband, whose work brought
us to Rota, and to our four beautiful children.
They have all been so patient as I made this idea a reality,
and let me work on it a few minutes
(or sometimes a few hours) at a time.

I also thank my Spanish friends who endured my questions
about food, culture, and travel with wonderful humor.

CONTENTS

PART I: GETTING SETTLED

PART II: SPANISH CULTURE

PART III: FOOD

PART IV: TRAVEL

DISCLAIMER

This book is intended to provide helpful information for families moving to Naval Station Rota. The advice in this book is researched and compiled by the author, without endorsement or regulation from Naval Station Rota officials. All information is based on the author's opinions and experience and is, to the author's knowledge, accurate as of August 2014. However, there may be discrepancies based on branch of military service, rank, or changes in base regulations or Spanish laws. In case of questions, always refer to your own chain of command or a representative of the Naval Station for an official response.

Wherever the star symbol appears, the information is based on material published by the Naval Station Rota Public Affairs Office, and available in the Welcome Aboard package.

PART I:

GETTING SETTLED

Overseas Screening Process
What to Pack: Express and Household Goods Shipments
Shipping a Vehicle to Spain
Items to Hand Carry
Passports
Save Money Before You Move
PCSing With Pets
Flying With Pets on Mac Flights
Flying Pets Commercially Through Madrid
Temporary Housing
Intercultural Relations (ICR) Class
Rental Cars and Buying Vehicles
Driving in Spain
Introduction to the Base
Base Services and Organizations
Technology: Phones, Internet, and Television
Employment
Housing Options
Towns Around Base
Should I Live On Base or In Town?
Hosting Guests On Base
Concrete Walls
School Opportunities

So you have orders to move your family to Rota, Spain. Congratulations! The process probably seems both exciting and daunting. This book will share my experiences moving to Rota, as well as some of the tips and downfalls experienced by my friends. Remember that everyone's experience is different. Wherever possible, I will direct you to the official information published on websites by the Naval Base. Websites will be updated more frequently, so even if my printed recommendations become outdated, websites and people currently living on base can give you more accurate answers.

Your greatest resource in preparing for a move will be your sponsor. You should be contacted by a sponsor who currently works at Naval Station Rota, and they will be able to answer specific questions about your future military unit, moving, housing, schools, the base, and activities. If you have not yet heard from a sponsor, contact the military unit to which you will be assigned in Rota. The chain of command can help ensure communication between you and your sponsor. Remember that a sponsor can only answer the questions you ask, so try to get in contact early and often. Don't hesitate to email questions about the base, living in Europe, etc. Put your spouse in touch with the sponsor's spouse so they can ask questions too! The sponsor can let you know how to prepare for your move, and what to expect when you arrive. They also prepare for your arrival by making arrangements for temporary housing, temporary furniture, a rental car, and giving you a ride from the airport. This can go a long way to reduce stress and help you adapt quickly to life in Spain.

Other resources available to you include the Ombudsmen, who are volunteer spouses from each unit on base. They ensure communication between families and the chain of command. The NAVSTA Ombudsmen maintain an official Facebook page under the name Naval Station Rota Ombudsman. The base Command sponsors its own official Facebook page under the name U.S. Naval Station Rota, Spain. There is also an unofficial Facebook page called Rota Community Q&A which can be a good resource for people moving here, or already stationed here, trying to get a quick answer from the general community. It is possible to reach out to the community and make some friends even before you arrive.

A great resource to get you started is the Welcome Aboard package, published by the Public Affairs Office of Naval Station Rota. This is a free online pamphlet that gives a general overview to the base, and addresses some of the logistical aspects of a military move. It is available at:

http://issuu.com/navstarota/docs/ welcome_aboard_package_2013.

The official website for Naval Station Rota is:

http://www.cnic.navy.mil/regions/cnreurafswa/ installations/ns_rota.html

OVERSEAS MEDICAL SCREENING PROCESS

This is a very important process to begin as soon as you receive orders. Rota has its own Naval Hospital on base, as well as programs like the Exceptional Family Member Program (EFMP) and Educational and Developmental Intervention Services (EDIS); however, it is a small base with a limited medical staff, so certain specialists are not available here. That means that every family receiving orders to Rota must go through the medical screening process for each family member BEFORE they move, to make sure that their needs can be accommodated during your tour. Pre-existing conditions or past surgeries, even if they are handled well at your current duty station, may make a family exempt from accompanying their service member overseas. Whether it is a chronic condition, a mental or learning disability, or a behavioral ailment, all concerns must be screened to see if needs can be met at Naval Station Rota. If you are on prescription medicine regularly, the military wants to make sure you will have access to your meds at all times, even if delivery is temporarily disrupted by weather or political situations.

Contact your chain of command at your current location to find out details about the screening process. Be honest, ask questions of your current doctor, and ask questions of your sponsor and the Naval Hospital Rota if you have any concerns. You do NOT want to find out when you've already moved here that certain physical, behavioral, or educational specialists are not available on this base, because then there is a chance of the family having to separate from their service member! Once you have your completed overseas screening paperwork, it should be hand-carried during your move, so that you can turn it in as soon as you arrive on base.

Your screening process will also ensure that all shots are up-to-date so you can be cleared for international travel. If you are not sure which shots you have received, a simple blood test at your current military hospital can determine what you need. Obtain and save hard copies of your children's shot and medical records from their current doctor and dentist.

When medical emergencies or injuries happen during your tour in Rota, some procedures can be handled in Rota's Naval Hospital emergency room, others will be referred to Spanish specialists in town, and serious conditions may require treatment at the larger American military bases in Germany. Tricare insurance will continue to cover you in those situations, which will be discussed more later.

> **Details about the Overseas Suitability Screening process and physical or mental conditions requiring an inquiry can be found on the Naval Hospital's website:**
>
> **http://www.med.navy.mil/sites/nhrota/Staff/Pages/OverseasScreening.aspx**

WHAT TO PACK

EXPRESS SHIPMENT:

A military move overseas is a similar process to any other permanent change of duty station (PCS) in some ways. Of course, you won't have the option to conduct a do-it-yourself move. But the military will reimburse moving expenses, including the moving company, packing supplies, and equipment rentals. You must go through DPS/PPSO at your current station, and schedule you move on www.move.mil. They will help you contact a moving company approved through your local base, one that is familiar with military moves. To prepare for your move, you must first determine which items to take as luggage on your plane ride, which to send in your Express Shipment (Unaccompanied Baggage), and which to pack up with the rest of your Household Goods (HHG). The Express Shipment can be packed up a few weeks ahead of your regular household goods shipment, and sent ahead so that it should arrive in country around the same time you do. The weight limit for the express shipment depends on rank and family size, but is typically rather low and does not include large items or furniture. The express shipment will be your only personal supplies for your first few weeks in Spain, besides whatever you carry in your luggage on the plane. When you first arrive, you will be placed in temporary housing, so it is good to consider whether you will be in the Navy Lodge (which is like a hotel), in an off-base hotel, or in an actual full-sized house on base. Temporary housing is discussed more later in this chapter.

Here are recommendations for your Express Shipment:

- Include clothing, shoes, and jackets for all family members. Consider what temperature changes will occur in the month following your move. (Seasons are discussed on page 70).
- Include cooking utensils and supplies. Your temporary housing will include a small kitchen, so packing 1 large pot, 1 frying pan, 1 bowl, 1 baking dish, 1 sharp knife, and a can opener at minimum will allow you to prepare some meals in your room.
- Include towels, bed sheets, and blankets for each person. You might not need these in the Navy Lodge, but you would in the other temporary housing, and since they are light weight, it will be better to have them than to buy new right away.
- If you are moving during summer, send your beach chairs, umbrella, towels, and beach toys express so you can go to the beaches as soon as you arrive!
- Send cleaning supplies like a vacuum, broom, dustpan, and mop.
- Baby gear like a Pack and Play, high chairs, cribs, swing, strollers, etc. can be included in the express shipment.
- Depending on the moving company policies, 1 TV can be included in this shipment.
- Desktop Computer, PlayStation, Xbox etc. can be sent, along with games and accessories.
- A small selection of toys, movies, or books should be included to entertain the family.
- Air mattress, area rugs, trash cans, shower curtains, hangers, and a floor lamp will make life in your temporary house more comfortable.
- Bikes should be included, if you have one, because it will give you a cheap transportation option when you arrive.
- Send a small set of screwdrivers, wrenches, hammers, nails, and scissors so that you can do any minor household jobs before your household good arrive, and so that you don't have to go through your whole shipment looking for the tools to open the boxes!
- Keep in mind that your temporary quarters may be small if you are in the Navy Lodge. Don't include furniture or excess items.
- Do NOT include any food, batteries, liquids, or hazardous materials in your shipment.

HOUSEHOLD GOODS SHIPMENT:

On the day of your main pack-out, a team of movers will come and pack up your entire house. You do not need to do much to prepare for them. Do not seal any boxes or wrap any items, as they are required to re-pack and wrap everything. You may want to gather similar items from around the house into one place, so that all books, picture frames, holiday decorations, or hobby supplies for example are packed together, but that is optional. The movers will label each box by the room it is currently in, with a very brief description of contents. You are allowed to go behind and write more detailed information on the box, to make things easier to find. Tell movers which items are high value, so they can be labeled appropriately on the "high value inventory." It is recommended that you write precise and detailed descriptions for electronics and valuable items. For example, CD's and DVD's should be counted by number, the TV box should have the brand and serial number of the TV, and computers should have a brand and serial number, rather than just saying "electronics." The movers will disassemble each piece of furniture to make it lay completely flat, and save the hardware in a separate box, or you can ask that hardware be put in a plastic bag and taped to each piece of furniture. Every item in the house will be at packed, so be sure to keep your personal items like I.D. cards, phone, computer, and purse in your car to avoid having them accidentally packed! Any luggage you intend to take on the plane should be put in an empty, clearly-labeled area so that it will not be packed. You can use a cleaned-out closet or bathroom for this.

Shipments from the East Coast often take 50-60 days to arrive in Spain. From the West Coast, times are usually 70-80 days. From Hawaii or Japan, it can take up to 120 days.

Appliances and Tools: You can send all your current small appliances in your Household Goods shipment, if you choose to bring them. Whether you live on or off base, you will be able to use them. Off base, it is easiest for appliances that can switch between 110 and 220 volts. If the appliance is dual voltage, it will say 110v- 240v on back of appliance. Phone chargers, TVs, and computers usually have this ability, but other small appliances like hair dryers, toasters, lamps, and vacuums do not. Small motors should be 50-60 hertz. If you are planning to live off base, you *can* use these items with a transformer, but it is usually better to purchase small appliances here so you don't have to plug into a transformer every time. You can always resell them before you move again. But if you haven't decided where to live, go ahead and bring small electronics and appliances. You do NOT need to send large appliances like a microwave, dishwasher, or freezer, as these are available from the Housing office for free. You also do NOT need to send American laundry washers and dryers. Base housing already includes a washer and dryer, and Self-Help will provide one if necessary for off-base accommodations. There is no hobby shop on base, so you should bring any specialty tools with you. Basic power tools and lawn equipment can be borrowed at no cost from the Self Help store on base, so it is optional whether you bring those tools.

Furniture and Rugs: Houses both on and off base usually have all tile floors, so bring any large area rugs or smaller throw rugs that you already have. You will need them! You may even want to purchase rugs before you move, since the selection when you first move is generally limited to what is available at the NEX or Ikea. On base, the newly-renovated 4-bedroom homes are spacious and have plenty of room for all furniture, with indoor and outdoor storage too. However, the older 2 and 3-bedroom homes are more cramped. To see floor plans of base housing, check the Welcome Aboard packet: http://issuu.com/navstarota/docs/welcome_aboard_package_2013. Then choose carefully which furniture to bring with you, and which pieces to sell before the move. In general, rooms in Spanish homes off-base are small, so in some cases a King-sized bed or extra-long couch will not fit. However, if you like your furniture, and are prepared to shop around for a house that accommodates it, go ahead and bring it. It is not difficult to find a large home, if that is what you want. Furniture selection in Spain is limited, due to the lack of hardwood trees. And furniture from the NEX is limited and generally pricey. Overhead lighting is also limited, so bring floor lamps and table lamps. There is a thrift shop on base, as well as an active yard sale web site for the base, if you need to quickly find or sell some items.

Firearms: Military personnel of ranks E-5 and above are authorized to ship firearms to Spain. However, weapons must be registered with the Spanish government, and are usually stored at the base Security Office armory. See the Welcome Aboard packet to see which types are permitted.

Christmas decorations: If you live on base, you may put up any lights and decorations on the interior or exterior of your home, as long as they cause no damage. Off base, you would have to use 220 volt lights, so American lights will not work. Live Christmas trees are sold at *Viveros,* (garden centers), near the base. However, they are not well pruned or nearly as pretty as Americans are used to. Fake trees from the NEX are extremely expensive, so if you already have a fake tree, you should pack it. Also, bring your tree stand, as they seem to be difficult to find.

Non-Temporary Storage: If you have furniture or items you do not want to bring to Spain, but are not willing to sell, talk to the Transportation Office of your current duty station about non-temporary storage. This is a one-time move of certain items, and storage should be authorized for the complete length of your overseas stay. That way you don't need to fill up your Spanish home with things you don't need here, but your goods will be available to you when you return to the United States. There are no storage lockers or rental units available around Rota for storing items locally. Non-temporary storage items will count against your total weight allotment for your move.

> **More advice on what to bring and what to leave can be found on the Naval Station's Housing website:**
>
> http://www.cnic.navy.mil/regions/cnreurafswa/insta
> llations/ns_rota/ffr/housing_and_lodging/what-
> should-i-bring-.html

SHIPPING A VEHICLE TO SPAIN

Military orders typically permit you to ship one American-spec vehicle (POV) free of charge per overseas PCS. This can be a car, truck, or motorcycle. Any bike with an engine larger than 50 cc's will be counted as a POV. Vehicles with custom window tint or modified parts are not usually permitted. You have to use designated cities for shipping, so you may need to drive your vehicle to another state and rent a car for the return trip. This rental is not reimbursed by the military, so it is better if a friend can drive with you. It will take over a month to ship a car from the East Coast, and a few weeks longer from the West Coast. It is beneficial to ship your car BEFORE your PCS date. It is easier to borrow or rent a car in the States, when you have family and friends nearby, than it will be to borrow or rent a car during your first month in Spain. When deciding what to bring, remember that European cars (and parking spaces) are typically smaller, and that gas is more expensive in Europe. There are plenty of vans and SUV's on base, but fewer in town. Also, be careful of shipping a new vehicle, as you can expect some scratches and dents as a routine part of the European driving style. Newer cars under warranty from US dealers may not have their warranties honored in Spain, even from a European company like VW or BMW, so confirm warranty details before you leave. Maintenance and replacement parts for American model cars can be ordered through the base Autoport.

Up-to-date procedures for shipping a vehicle are outlined on the Naval Station Rota Relocation Assistance 'Automobiles' section. This provides details about shipping requirements, pick-up procedure, license, insurance, child seat guidelines, and even Moped information.

Please visit their page for official guidelines:

http://www.cnic.navy.mil/regions/ cnreurafswa/installations/ns_rota/ ffr/support_services/ relocation_assistance/automobiles.html.

WHEN WE SHIPPED A VEHICLE FROM THE STATES, HERE ARE THE STEPS WE FOLLOWED:

1. Before you leave the States, contact your insurance company to ask about international insurance. Most companies don't carry it, but USAA and Geico do. Explain that you are shipping your vehicle, and get the "green card" (Foreign Insurance document) before you go. Make sure there is no lapse of coverage in your insurance dates. Your vehicle insurance and registration must be up-to-date when the vehicle ARRIVES in Spain, so be sure to renew before shipping, if necessary. Photograph your car to document any pre-existing damage, or its current pristine condition. Leave your state license plates on the vehicle, so you can temporarily drive it in Spain. If the VPC takes them off, ask for them to be sent with the vehicle, or pack them in your suitcase. (You can mail them back to your state later, if required).

2. When you ship your vehicle, keep all relevant documents—Title, Registration, foreign insurance card, and shipping records—in a safe place in your hand-carried items. You don't want these to get lost in the move, or risk them showing up later than your car! During your check-in process, contact the Vehicle Processing Center (VPC) located off base in Puerto, and let them know how to contact you when your vehicle arrives. It takes about 5-6 weeks to ship a car from the east coast, longer from the West Coast.

3. Eventually, you will get an e-mail from the VPC that your car is HERE! Before you can get it you have to jump through some hoops. They will send a customs document (*Conduce*) to the Security Office on base. Go to the Security Office with your I.D. and your vehicle's stateside registration, and pick up the *Conduce*.

4. You will need to pay a vehicle registration fee of around 100 Euros. (2014 price, subject to change) Either get Euros from the ATM at Banco Popular, or go to PSD either to have dollars changed into Euros, or to write a check and have it cashed. Then take your Euros to the Banco Popular on base, and get a receipt for the registration fee.

5. Take the *Conduce* and the stateside registration to the service station on base, and schedule a safety inspection (ITV). They will give you a form confirming your appointment.

6. Go back to Security. This step must be completed by the military Sponsor IN PERSON, and they must have all of the following documents: Bank receipt of the registration fee, form confirming safety inspection appointment, 3 copies of military orders, stateside registration form, international insurance (green card), Spanish drivers' license (the test is given during ICR) or a translated copy of your stateside license. If you have all of this, Security will give you a release form to go get your vehicle, as well as a temporary pass to drive the vehicle on base.

7. Go pick up your vehicle. The Vehicle Processing Center is in Puerto. As long as the stateside license plates are still on, you can drive the vehicle with those plates for one month. Keep the vehicle pass Security gave you displayed in your window to gain entrance to base.

8. Take the vehicle to the base Autoport for the ITV inspection. This is a safety inspection, not a mechanical test. They are mostly checking for custom body work, tinted windows, non-standard wheel sizes, etc. (None of these things are allowed in Spain). In order to pass the ITV, you must first purchase: 1 safety vest, 2 reflective triangles, and replacement light bulbs. These items are available in the Auto center (about $25), and they will even look up your light bulb specs. The vehicle should be dropped off by 8:45 the morning of inspection, and will be ready around 1pm. The inspection costs $45. You will receive an ITV card stating that you passed the inspection.

9. Take the ITV card to the Vehicle Registration Section of Security, so they can process the Spanish registration.

10. Once Security receives the Registration, you will go to Security to pick it up. It will have your new license plate number on it. Contact your insurance company with this info.

11. Go to the Autoport on base to order your license plates. Bring your Spanish Registration showing the license number. The plates cost $22 per set, plus $8.50 to have them installed. (2014 prices, subject to change). The plates don't come with holes drilled, so if you don't pay installation you will have to drill them yourself.

Done! Now you have an American vehicle that is legally insured, registered, and licensed in Spain! You will have to submit it for annual ITV inspections, but you will not pay the Spanish tax (VAT) since it was not purchased here.

ITEMS TO HAND-CARRY

These are the things you will pack with you on the plane, to have available as soon as you arrive on base. Essential documents should be in a carry-on bag, not a checked bag, in case baggage is lost during your travels. You may want to organize them all into a binder to keep everything from getting crushed, and make it easy to flip through documentation.

Have the following documents on hand when you arrive to assist with your family's check-in process:

- Passport (no-fee passport is required for each dependent, tourist passport optional)
- Original and multiple copies of orders. Depending on branch, ensure the orders correctly list dependents
- Valid military I.D. for active duty and dependents
- Overseas Screening Paperwork for all family members
- Medical Records
- Birth Certificates, Social Security cards, and other I.D.
- Up-to-date Shot Records for children, and current LES (Leave and Earnings Statement) to register at school or CDC
- Travel Itinerary and all travel receipts, to receive reimbursement
- Vehicle title, insurance, registration, shipping documents, and keys, so you can pick up your vehicle when it arrives.

PASSPORTS

Military personnel stationed overseas and their dependent family members may qualify for a 'no-fee' passport, which should be applied for at least 3 months before your move. These are free, because the military handles the application process and the fees. You will need to coordinate the application process with your current command's PSD or Admin Office, and provide photos and documents in a timely manner. You do not need a Spanish Visa when moving under military orders. The no-fee passport is required to enter another country (Spain) under military orders. However, the no-fee passport should not be used for private travel or vacations, so in order to fly anywhere in Europe or check into hotels, a regular tourist passport is necessary for all family members. These can be acquired once stationed in Spain, but it is MUCH easier and faster to apply for them in the States before you move. You can apply at your local post office or passport center. You will be responsible for the application fees, and will not be reimbursed. Passports typically cost over $100 per person. It takes 6-8 weeks to receive a passport after you submit the application, so apply well in advance of your travel dates. Applications can be expedited for a high fee.

The *entrada*, or entry Visa, is stamped into dependents' no-fee passport. The Security Office keeps your passport for about 10 days, then returns it with the stamp. Upon arrival, you will be issued a Spanish I.D. card at the Security office. This is used to move on and off base, so you only need to carry your passport when you travel.

For details on tourist passport applications, go to the Department of State's website:
http://travel.state.gov/passport.html.

Tourist passport information can also be found at:
http://cnic.navy.mil/regions/cnreurafswa/installations/ns_rota/about/departments/administration.html

No-fee passport information can be found at:
http://cnic.navy.mil/regions/cnreurafswa/installations/ns_rota/about/tennant_commands/personnel-support-activity-europe--detachment-rota--psd--/passport-information.html.

SAVE MONEY BEFORE YOU MOVE

Moving a family to another country is a long and costly process. While the military does cover many moving expenses—moving company, shipping a vehicle, airfare, per diem stipends for food and hotels, and even a "redecorating allowance"—there are also many hidden costs. We had money saved, and didn't have any major mishaps, but we were still amazed by the amount of money needed to start up life here. Estimates vary, but to be comfortable, a family should save at least $4,000 to prepare for an overseas military move.

Even though certain travel items like airfare and hotel lodging might be 'covered for reimbursement' from the military, you still need to pay for them out of pocket. You save your receipts, submit a claim, and then can wait several weeks for your request to be accepted. You are going to have to make that credit card payment before the military money actually hits your account. So you need to have several paychecks worth of liquid savings ready to handle the unusual expenses. And if you travel on anything besides your approved dates (i.e. staying in a hotel while checking out of a duty station, or while travelling to visit family) those expenses won't be reimbursed at all because they are not on the actual PCS dates.

If you decide to rent a house or apartment in Spain, be prepared to pay two months' rent up front (1 payment for the first month, 1 for the security deposit), and don't count on receiving your security deposit back. If you continue to own and rent out your stateside property, be prepared to pay several months' mortgage out of pocket, in case renters are not immediately found.

In addition, there are going to be unexpected expenses: rental car, clothing, food, comfort purchases. All those liquids, flammables, batteries, and compressed items that the moving company wouldn't ship will have to be re-purchased. Your kitchen pantry will have to be restocked. And you will have to purchase household goods to accommodate your new home layout, number of bathrooms, etc. You may purchase replacement furniture or a second vehicle. A GPS and cell phone are essential purchases. (An American GPS will not work in Europe unless you have paid to download the European maps. Try this before you move. An American cell phone will only work if it is unlocked and has a European SIM card. You can do that in advance or when you arrive.) When you first arrive in Spain, you don't know good stores, and you aren't sure what a competitive price is, so you are stuck paying whatever the NEX tells you is a fair deal. So, once again: be prepared for enormous credit card bills, and have a plan for paying them off.

Be prepared for huge inconsistencies in the military paycheck. There are a lot of adjustments that need to be made during a PCS move, and sometimes they don't get changed correctly in the computer payment system. So check your pay schedule repeatedly, and see if it is accurately reflecting your situation. BAH will stop when you check out of your current duty station. Overseas Housing Allowance (OHA) will start when you sign a lease for an off-base house here. The cost-of-living allowance (COLA) in Spain is based on rank and family size. The good news is that anything the military owes you they will eventually give you when you make a correction request. But it is your responsibility to stay on top of it, and be prepared for adjustments to take several pay cycles to get worked out. Going several paychecks in a row missing a few hundred dollars really affects the budget! Also, anything you owe the military they will eventually take back. So if you got advance pay before the move, or if they somehow overpaid you in some of the PCS calculations, you may suddenly receive a paycheck much lower than usual because they subtracted what you 'owe.' That's why it is so important to have extra liquid savings to get through paycheck fluctuations.

Finally, closing out your former billing accounts can be expensive. When you leave the States, it is your responsibility to schedule cancellation of water, electricity, cable, internet, security system, cell phones, and car insurance bills. Most companies make you pay the final balance immediately upon cancellation, no matter where you are in the billing cycle. Others mail a bill later asking for a cancellation fee. Some make you pay ahead into the next billing cycle before processing the cancellation request. So your 'typical' monthly bills will be completely unpredictable for a month or so. Always ask if the company has a military clause to let you out of a contract early.

Moving is a long process—it takes months, not weeks. And it is expensive, even if the military supposedly covers most of it. So plan ahead, but most of all be prepared with lots of liquid savings. USAA and the Navy-Marine Corps Relief Society offer low interest or even interest-free loans if you get into a tight spot.

PCSing WITH PETS

Pets are permitted to travel overseas with their family, but there are numerous guidelines and restrictions you should be aware of before you move. Transporting a pet is costly—sometimes $1,000 or more per animal—so begin saving well before your moving date. Expenses to move a pet are not covered or reimbursed by the military. Remember that you will have to pay for the shipping process once again when moving a pet from Rota to the United States. Never abandon an animal. If you cannot bring it with you for any reason, or cannot pay round-trip expenses, arrange for a new family to adopt it. If you do not yet have a pet, there are numerous opportunities to get one in Spain. The shelter on base, RAWL (Rota Animal Welfare League), arranges adoptions for cats and dogs. There are also pedigree breeding centers throughout Spain.

In on-base housing, there is a limit of two pets (dogs or cats) per household. Off base, many homes are pet-friendly. When deciding how many pets to bring, remember to consider the round-trip costs of transporting them. Notify your sponsor if you are bringing pets, so they can make appropriate reservations in temporary lodging.

The Naval Station Rota Relocation Assistance Office can answer your questions about current pet guidelines and procedures. These are outlined on their website:

http://www.cnic.navy.mil/regions/cnreurafswa/ installations/ns_rota/ffr/support_services/ relocation_assistance/pets.html

Another good resource is the base Veterinarian. You must register pets with the base Vet within 15 days of arrival. Currently, they maintain their official Facebook page under the name: Rota Branch Veterinary Treatment Facility.

REQUIREMENTS FOR IMPORTING DOGS AND CATS

The entry of dogs, cats, or ferrets under three months of age is not allowed. All animals must be identified with a 15-digit microchip to be registered in the Spanish database, which should ideally be obtained in the States, but can be obtained on base upon arrival if necessary. The Rabies vaccine must be administered AFTER the microchip and then a period of 21 days should follow before entering into Spain. For booster vaccinations, no waiting period is required, provided the booster vaccine was administered before the expiration date of the prior vaccine.

Animals must be accompanied by a veterinary certificate, issued by an Official Veterinarian, (your current base Veterinarian or military-approved Veterinarian), which will include the following:
- Identification of the owner or person responsible for the animal(s)
- Description and origin of the animal(s)
- Microchip number, location and date of insertion.
- Information on the rabies vaccine (the vaccine type must be inactive, and in compliance with the standards of the OIE).

The Veterinary certificate is valid within 10 days of arrival into the country. Animals without the certificate will be denied entry into Spain. After arrival, pets must be registered with the base veterinarian within 15 days. If you travel with your pet within Europe, they will need a pet passport, which will be part of the registration process when you check in with the base Veterinarian.

This information was obtained from the Office of Agriculture, Food, and Environment of the Spanish Embassy in Washington, D.C. Further details are available on their website:

http://www.mapausa.org/eng/nc_2.htm

'POTENTIALLY DANGEROUS' DOGS

This information was obtained from the Office of Agriculture, Food, and Environment of the Spanish Embassy in Washington, D.C. Further details are available on their website:

http://www.mapausa.org/eng/nc_3.htm.

Certain breeds of dogs are deemed 'potentially dangerous' by the Spanish government. These breeds are: Pit Bull Terrier, Staffordshire Bull Terrier, American Staffordshire Terrier, Rottweiler, Dogo Argentino, Fila Brasileiro, Tosa Inu, Akita Inu, and crosses of these breeds. Legally, they can be imported, but the owner must adhere to Spanish laws, which include obtaining a license, paying a fee, obtaining insurance, and passing a psychological exam.

Before you leave the United States:
1. Obtain veterinary certificate
2. Obtain certification of owner's police record

Once in Spain:
1. Obtain certificate of physical ability;
2. Obtain certificate of psychological aptitude;
3. Purchase liability insurance;
4. Apply for registration at the Town or City Registry of Potentially Dangerous Animals and obtain the license.
5. Comply at all times with the safety measures.

Potentially dangerous dogs must be identified with a microchip. They also must be registered in the Town or City Registries of Potentially Dangerous Animals. The dog owner must have a license, issued by the municipality, valid for five years. In order to qualify for a license, the owner must meet the following requirements:

- Must be 18 years or older.
- Must have a clean police record showing no convictions for the crimes of homicide, torture, assault, sex-related offenses, drug trafficking, association with illegal armed groups, or otherwise having been banned by court order of the right to own potentially dangerous animals. These requirements must be documented with the appropriate certificates issued by the police authorities with jurisdiction over the owner's place(s) of residence during the two years prior to the application for license.
- Must be mentally and physically able to own and control potentially dangerous animals. This requirement will be documented with the appropriate certificates (certificate of physical aptitude and certificate of psychological aptitude) issued by authorized centers in Spain.
- Must have proof of contract of an insurance policy on the animal(s) with liability coverage of at least 120,000 Euros.

FLYING WITH PETS ON MAC FLIGHTS

Pet transportation varies, depending if your family is flying commercial or using the military Patriot Express (Rotator) flights. One big difference: The commercial airline industry currently imposes a 100 pound weight restriction per pet with kennel. They also impose a restriction on pet shipments during seasonal hot/cold conditions. These industry restrictions should be considered when making

> This information is from the Pet Travel Brochure, published by Air Mobility Command, and available online at:
>
> **http://www.amc.af.mil/ shared/media/document/ AFD-131011-020.pdf**

pet travel plans. AMC (The Rotator) has a weight limit of 150 pounds per pet with kennel. There are usually spaces available on the rotator to ship animals here, but space is much more limited when returning from Spain to the United States. The Animal Welfare Act limits Patriot Express flights to 10 pet spaces per rotator flight.

You are responsible to ensure pets are shipped in the strongest and most secure kennel you can find. To prevent potential delays in your travel on major air carriers, two piece kennels should be bolted together with metal bolts and nuts.

Fees are charged on a weight per kennel basis. Your pet(s) and kennel with combined weight up to 70 pounds will be charged as one piece of checked luggage. Pet(s) and kennel with combined weight from 71-140 pounds will be charged as two pieces of checked luggage, and pet(s) and kennel weighing from 141-150 pounds will be charged as three pieces of checked luggage. Pet(s) and kennel weighing in excess of 150 pounds will not be accepted for shipment under any circumstances.

If the ground time exceeds 2 hours, pets will be off-loaded and owners will be provided an opportunity to visit their pets. When passengers are allowed to disembark from an aircraft due to flight delay, pet owners will also be provided an opportunity to visit their pets in order to walk them and provide water. Currently, Spain does not require a quarantine period for imported pets.

For the rotator, DOD regulations limit pet shipment to passengers in PCS status only. Pet space is limited on all AMC Patriot

Express flights, therefore pet spaces are booked on a first come, first serve basis. You are limited to two pets per family. Pets must be accompanied by their owner and shipment is at the owners' expense.

Contact your local transportation office as early as possible to book your pet space. Please remember, you are responsible for obtaining all required documentation, immunization, and border clearance requirements.

> **To fly, your dog will need an EU health certificate which you can print online:**
>
> http://www.aphis.usda.gov/regulations/vs/ iregs/animals/downloads/sp_no_com_pe.pdf
>
> **and an international health certificate which your Vet should have:**
>
> http://www.aphis.usda.gov/library/forms/pdf/AP HIS7001.pdf

Forms must be filled out by an NVAP accredited vet, then signed by an Official Veterinary employed by the Veterinary Services, Animal and Plant Health Inspection Service (VS/APHIS). The easiest way to do this is to use a military Vet who can fill out the forms as both a NVAP and VS/APHIS Vet. Otherwise, you will need to have your Vet fill out the forms, then either find your local APHIS office and make an appointment to have your forms signed, or mail your forms to APHIS with a prepaid return envelope. APHIS charges about $25 to sign forms. Once your Vet fills out the health certificate it is only good for 10 days and must still be valid when your dog arrives in Spain, so this will all need to be done fairly quickly.

With any questions, contact the Vet clinic on base in Rota. You will have to check your pet in there within 15 days of arrival. Your pet needs to be registered in the Spanish database, regardless of where they will be treated. If you fly with a pet on a commercial flight within Europe, you will need to acquire a pet passport. The Vet office on base can assist you with that process when you check in. Spain determines the registration fees, which in 2014 were about $25.

FLYING PETS COMMERCIALLY THROUGH MADRID

Note: The author did not ship pets, so this section was contributed by Jessica and Andrew Strong..

PRE PCS

If there is a chance your dog won't be able to travel with you on the MAC flight, make arrangements ahead of time to ship the dog commercially. It will make your life easier and cost less money than if you have to scramble to make arrangements 15 days prior to PCS. Make sure your kennel meets international requirements. These are listed on airline websites. Make sure you know your dog's weight, kennel's weight, and kennel measurements.

THINGS TO CONSIDER

Not all planes are large enough to accommodate medium and larger kennels. You will probably have to ship from an international airport to Madrid, not a local airport with connecting flights. If you are having someone else watch and ship your dog to you, make sure they live near a major international airport or are willing to drive to one. If you are already in Rota, make arrangements to drive to Madrid, since your pet probably won't be able to get any closer. There are courier services that will drive the animals from Madrid or from Malaga to Rota, but you can also rent a car and get them yourself. Driving to Malaga takes about 3 hours. Madrid takes about 6-7 hours, so you may need overnight accommodations.

Many airlines have temperature restrictions. Most won't transport pets during the summer but there are also cold requirements too. For example, American Airlines won't fly pets if it's below 45. United Petsafe (1-800-575-3335) is easy to deal with, well informed, friendly, and their cargo hold is climate controlled so they will fly pets when others won't. There are also breed restrictions, particularly with snub-nosed dogs and cats.

Don't just make arrangements on-line! Call people several times to confirm everything.

> **To fly, your dog will need an EU health certificate which you can print online:**
>
> http://www.aphis.usda.gov/regulations/vs/ iregs/animals/downloads/sp_no_com_pe.pdf
>
> **and an international health certificate which your Vet should have:**
>
> http://www.aphis.usda.gov/library/forms/pdf/APHIS 7001.pdf

THE PROCESS

Your dog needs a 15 digit ISO standard microchip and a yearly rabies vaccination. If your dog must get the microchip it will also need another rabies vaccination. Good places for info are www.mapausa.org and www.aphis.usda.gov/. There you can get the full list of requirements.

Make flight arrangements. The cost may be around $1,000 or more based on your dog's weight and kennel size. You pay when you drop the dog off so you can always change this flight if you need too. Forms must be filled out by an NVAP accredited Vet then signed by an Official Veterinary employed by the Veterinary Services, Animal and Plant Health Inspection Service (VS/APHIS). The easiest way to do this is to use a military Vet who can fill out the forms as both a NVAP and VS/APHIS Vet. If this option is not possible you will need to have your Vet fill out the forms then either find your local APHIS office and make an appointment to have your forms signed or mail your forms to APHIS with a prepaid return envelope. APHIS charges about $25 to sign forms. Once your Vet fills out the health certificate it is only good for 10 days and must still be valid when your dog arrives in Spain.

The next step is to put your dog on a plane. Check with the airline for pre-flight requirements. The typical is food/water/potty no more than 4 hours before. You can tape a Ziploc bag to the top of the kennel for food, leash and forms. The airlines provide live animal and arrow stickers as well as releasable cable ties for the door. Also check what time the dog needs to be dropped off. Typically it is 3 hours before an international flight, but check the times when the cargo facility opens. Call several times before you drop your dog off. If flights are rescheduled, you may have to redo the health certificate and EU form.

PICKING UP YOUR PET IN MADRID

Once in Madrid you will pick your dog up in the cargo area. Follow the signs for cargo near the airport. See an airport map here: http://www.aena-aeropuertos.es/csee/Satellite?Language=EN. You will need passport or I.D. to get in the gate, then tell the guard you're picking up a dog. Walk into the door at the front of the building and there is a counter. Whoever was listed as the recipient on the paperwork needs to be there with a passport to pick up the dog. You will pay about 72 Euros in fees and receive paperwork to take to the vet.

Next take your paperwork to the customs Vet. It's the big glass building on the corner. As you walk up to the building, there is an information desk in the middle where you will show your passport and get a card to gain access to the building. Tell them you need the Veterinarian and they can give you the floor and office number. The Vet will want passports and the paperwork the airline gave you. He will stamp and give you paperwork to give to customs.

Turn your card in at the info desk. As you walk back towards the road, customs is the glass doors now on your left (café on right). You will need to go through security/metal detector then head to the counter to the left. You can show your paperwork to security and they will point you in the right direction. Customs will want to know it's a pet, see your passport, take your paperwork and give you a form to fill out. When you're done you can head back to cargo area and pick up your pet!

TEMPORARY HOUSING

When you arrive, your sponsor should meet you at the airport and take you to your temporary housing. It is the sponsor's job to make arrangements for temporary housing, but you should confirm this ahead of time. There are several types of temporary housing, and it is hard to predict which you will have, since they are based on availability. You may stay up to 30 days after arrival, until you either select a house to rent in town, or sign up for base housing. Your express shipment should arrive shortly after you get here, so you can use expressed items at your temporary housing.

OPTION ONE: BASE HOUSING

Some families choose temporary lodging in base housing. It is not their permanent home, but it is a full-sized base house with kitchen, bedrooms, and bathrooms. Appliances such as washer, dryer, oven/stove, and refrigerator/freezer are included. Phone is provided, but internet is NOT available. If you need Internet access, the Liberty Center (MWR) and Library have computers. There is Wi-Fi available at Subway in the NEX, and Pizza Villa. The house will be completely empty. You or your sponsor can order temporary furniture through the housing office, at no cost, and keep it until you are assigned permanent quarters. Temporary furniture includes beds, tables, chairs, sofas, lamps, desks, etc. It is not comfortable, similar to the furniture found in a college dorm room, but it is better than nothing! The Fleet and Family Center also has packages of kitchen dishes, glasses, and cooking supplies that are available to borrow for free during your first month. Some military units also have sets available for new families, so check with your sponsor about how to get these supplies. There is no charge to stay in base housing, but you will not receive any housing compensation in your paycheck, either. Most pets are allowed in base housing, because all houses have fenced-in yards. The housing area on base is very close to the base school, but about two miles from most other base services such as Commissary, NEX, library, gym, restaurants, and the Rota gate. It is possible to bike or walk or take the on-base shuttle to these locations, but it is not very convenient. A rental car will be an important amenity if you stay in the base housing area and do not have your car.

OPTION TWO: THE NAVY LODGE

The Navy Lodge is basically an on-base hotel with different room configurations for individuals or families. The cost and the number of rooms allotted for a family are based on rank. Pets are not allowed in most rooms, or must be kept in a kennel at all times in others. Rooms include beds and kitchenette, refrigerator, microwave, basic cooking utensils, telephone, and a TV. Free Wi-Fi internet is available. Families are generally assigned to one room with two queen beds. The quarters may be cramped for a family, since children do not typically receive additional rooms. While staying in the Navy Lodge, you will receive a per diem payment based on rank, which will reimburse the cost of the stay and some food for up to 30 days. However, this reimbursement may not appear on your paycheck for several pay cycles, so be prepared to pay for the lodging out of pocket until you are reimbursed. The Lodge is conveniently located behind the Commissary and NEX, and is easy walking distance to base restaurants and other services. The school bus for the on-base school will stop at the Navy Lodge.

OPTION THREE: HOTEL IN TOWN

In rare cases when there is no temporary housing or rooms available on base, families will be placed in a hotel off base, in Rota or Puerto. You or the sponsor must obtain a certificate of non-availability from the Navy Lodge in order for you to stay in a hotel off base. The military will reimburse hotel costs as part of your moving expenses, but they will not reimburse the cost of a rental car. Your sponsor should make reservations for the hotel and a rental car. This would usually only be temporary until housing becomes available on base.

INTERCULTURAL RELATIONS CLASS (ICR)

Immediately upon arrival, all adults should be enrolled in the Intercultural Relations Class through the Fleet and Family Service Center. This is not just for military personnel, but for their spouses as well. Childcare is provided for free at the base CDC for children ages 5 and under (registration and reservations required in advance). Older children will be enrolled in school or—during the summer—in a youth summer camp. The classes are held in the Community Support building, near the Fleet and Family Service Center offices. During the summer PCS season, ICR is held every week, from Monday to Thursday. At other times of the year, it is offered every other week. Attendance should begin on Monday and continue until Thursday. The class meets from about 8:30am- 3:30pm.

During ICR, a huge amount of paperwork will be handled. Representatives from almost every organization on base—including Housing, Security, Schools, and the Hospital, will speak with you about necessary actions and assist you in completing enrollment paperwork. You will be able to ask questions and learn detailed steps of how to get settled. You will also learn some elementary Spanish, complete the written test to acquire a Spanish driver's license, and take a daytrip into Rota to explore the town and experience Spanish culture and food. Attendance is mandatory for military personal, and highly encouraged for spouses.

RENTAL CARS AND BUYING VEHICLES

RENTAL CARS:

Typically, families arriving in Rota need to rent a car for a short period of time, either until their own vehicle ships from the States, or until they are able to buy a car locally. Buying a car will take at least a few weeks, because you first need to acquire an N.I.E. (explained below) and that can take up to 1 month to process. Most rentals available in Europe are manual, stick-shift vehicles. Automatic transitions are harder to find, and will cost much more. (Which is why I learned to drive stick shift the day we arrived in Spain!) Vehicles can be rented from the air terminal on base (through NEX car rentals), from various companies in Rota, or from the airport in Jerez de la Frontera. Your sponsor can help with this process, and should make the arrangement ahead of your arrival. Prices vary, but are generally higher than American rates: $200-$400 per week (in 2014). Prices are discounted if the reservation is for an entire month.

BUYING A VEHICLE IN SPAIN:

If you choose to purchase a vehicle in Spain, you will have several options, but first you must be aware of the legal requirements: *Americans living in Spain are permitted to import 1 American-spec vehicle per PCS orders, and own 1 European-spec vehicle without paying the very high Spanish taxes. A motorcycle will count as a POV, so you can NOT import both a motorcycle and a car from the States.*
If you ship an American vehicle from the States, you will only be able to purchase a European-spec vehicle when you arrive here. While it is possible to buy a new car from one of many dealers in town, most people prefer not to get a brand new vehicle because of the likelihood of damage due to Spanish driving styles. Roads are narrow, parking spots are tight, and it is very common for vehicles to bump or scrape against each other without the driver stopping to assess damage. Usually, it is more beneficial to buy a used car on base. These are referred to as 'Rota beaters,' and range in make, mileage, and price. Used cars can be found in the lemon lot across from the base gym, advertised in The Coastline newspaper, or on the Rota

Yard Sales Facebook page. To purchase a vehicle, you must first have an N.I.E. (Spanish Identification Number), which can be obtained from the base Security Office. You must bring exact change of 13.36 Euros (2014 price) to the Banco Popular on base. They will give you a receipt. Bring the receipt, your Spanish I.D. card, American I.D. card, and passport to the Security Office to process an application. It will take several weeks to process the N.I.E, then you will receive a phone call from Security to pick it up.

Be aware that all cars driven in Spain must have passed an ITV safety inspection (available at the base Auto Port) and this inspection must be conducted every 1-2 years, depending on your car's age. So if you buy a car nearing or past its ITV inspection date, you will be responsible for the cost of the inspection, and any repairs needed to bring it up to code. If the ITV is up to date, new owners do not need to conduct it until the pass nears expiration.

You can also choose to purchase a motorcycle or moped after arriving in Spain. These can be purchased from outgoing service members or local nationals. Any bike with an engine larger than 50 cc's is considered a POV. American motorcycles must pass an ITV inspection on base. Spanish or European bikes must pass an ITV inspection off base.

To drive a motorcycle, you must document at least 2 prior years of having a motorcycle endorsement on a U.S. license before obtaining a Spanish motorcycle license. Motorcycle owners must take a motorcycle safety course, which is usually offered once a month on base through the Safety Office.

A bike with an engine smaller than 50 cc's is considered a moped. These are convenient on Spain's narrow streets, but also dangerous and have high insurance rates. A moped must remain in Spain, and cannot be shipped back to the United States upon departure. Mopeds are subject to an annual or semi-annual ITV inspection, but the ITV inspection centers for mopeds are located off-base.

DRIVING IN SPAIN

To drive in Spain, you must be 18 years old, and in possession of a Spanish Driver's license. When you first arrive, you can obtain a translation of your stateside driver's license (available from the base Security Department at no cost) to drive on and off-base. During ICR class, you will take a written test (in English) of European road signs and driving laws. You must pass this test in order to receive a temporary Driver's License, but the ICR teachers will spend some time preparing you for it. It then takes about two weeks to receive your permanent Spanish Driver's License. This license allows you to drive in any country in the European Union. Driving in other countries requires an International Driver's License.

A motorcycle license and a safety course, as mentioned previously, are required to drive a motorcycle larger than 50 cc's. To receive a motorcycle license, you must document having a motorcycle license for at least two years prior.

The Spanish drive on the same side of the road as Americans, but use different road signs, and speed limits are all listed in kilometers per hour. Additionally, the Spanish have fewer traffic lights, and many roundabouts, so directions can be confusing at first. Roads in many towns, including Rota, are very narrow, and one-way streets are frequent. A GPS is an essential tool, but even with one, driving off base and exploring new areas requires courage and steady nerves. However, most Americans quickly adjust to driving on and off base, and it does not affect their daily routines.

Traffic is not a problem in the towns around the Naval base. There is some congestion in downtown areas, but there are no rush hour traffic jams. Getting off base around 2 pm (siesta time) is slow, but other times traffic is light. Highway speeds are slightly higher than in the States.

GENERAL ADVICE FOR ROAD RULES:

- Do not use a cell phone while driving. Use of a hand-held device while driving is prohibited on and off base.
- Pedestrians always have the right of way, especially in crosswalks (even though they don't always use them.) People will step right off the curb into traffic and expect you to stop, so always stay alert and drive cautiously in urban areas.
- In roundabouts, use the outer lane if you are taking the first or second exit, and the inner lane if you are going further around the circle. Always exit from the outer-most lane. (But be aware that the Spanish don't always follow this rule!)
- Always use your turn signal when turning or changing lanes, including in a roundabout.
- If you miss a turn, don't make a U-turn. Either continue to go around the circle until you find your exit, or continue on the road until you come to the next roundabout and are able to change direction safely.
- The left lane is generally for passing, or for faster traffic. Slower traffic should always keep to the right.
- Headlights should be turned on in tunnels, no matter how short they are.
- Do not make a right turn when a traffic light is red, even if the road is clear. Wait for the light to turn green before turning.
- Child car seat laws are similar to the States, and based on child's age and weight. Children under 12 should not be in the front seat, even in a taxi.
- Do not park in areas with a yellow or red curb.
- Parking is permitted in blue spaces, but these usually require payment, especially during summer months. Look for an automated payment kiosk nearby.

Pay close attention to speed limits, both on and off base. Highways frequently have speed cameras which automatically photograph your license plate and send you a ticket, even if you are only a few kilometers over the limit. Traffic tickets in Spain can be issued for speeding or for any traffic violation. The tickets usually carry very heavy fines, much higher than rates seen in America. For a minor offense such as missing a taillight or parking in a non-designated area, the fine is 80 Euros. For a major offense, such as speeding or failure to stop, the fine is 200 Euros. For a very serious offense like driving while intoxicated or excessive speed, the fine can be 500 Euros, and up to 1,000 Euros for a repeat offense. If you pay within 20 days, you only have to pay 50% of the fine listed. If you wait until after that to pay or appeal, you will have to pay the full amount. You can also pay on the scene when the officer issues the ticket to take advantage of the 50% discount.

When biking, be aware of surrounding traffic, and either use designated paths on the sidewalk, or ride on the shoulder. All bikers, including children, must wear helmets at all times. Infant seats attached to a bike are permitted throughout Spain, as long as the bike operator is at least 18 years old. Bike trailers pulled behind a bike are technically not legal, according to Spanish law. However, you will see them sold and used in some areas, because town halls have the right to permit them in each town or in public parks. In Rota, they are not officially allowed. On base, they are permitted.

INTRODUCTION TO THE BASE

Naval Station Rota is first of all a Spanish naval base. Although many Americans are stationed here, it is not controlled by the American military. There is an extension of the SOFA (Status of Forces Agreement) called the Agreement on Defensive Cooperation that determines the rights and limitations for Americans living here. Americans must adhere to Spanish laws, including traffic regulations. The base is not 'American soil' like an embassy compound, so babies born here will be issued American birth abroad certificates. Americans must always be aware of the privilege of living and working on base, and must show respect for the Spanish military.

On base, there are numerous commands, not only from the Spanish military, but from the American Navy, Air Force, Army, and Marines. For some military families, this may be their first time living on a Navy base, and it is normal to have neighbors from various military branches. For the most part, cooperation between branches is excellent, and the Rota community is welcoming and helpful regardless of your branch of service. Remember that it is a small and tight-knit community. Often, this is positive because people really do help each other and welcome newcomers. But it can be negative if you allow trivial problems to become major ordeals. Try to reserve judgments and not burn bridges when you first arrive. Your family will probably spend several years here in the base community.

The currency used on base is Dollars, so don't get rid of your American money before you move! Commissary and NEX prices are listed in Dollars only, and bills for base services are also in Dollars. It is easy to convert between Dollars and Euros at Personnel Support Detachment (PSD) or the NEX Customer Service desk. You can convert cash, or cash a check into Dollars at those locations. There are also certain ATM's—like at the Banco Popular—that dispense either Dollars or Euros. You do not need an account with the Banco Popular to use their ATM. Off base, the currency is the Euro, and Dollars will not be accepted.

Water on base is safe to drink in all buildings. It is tested regularly to ensure that it meets American water quality standards. The water does not contain Fluoride, but the base Dentist can prescribe Fluoride drops. Some people choose to filter tap water with a Brita or similar filter, but that is simply a matter of taste.

BASE SERVICES AND ORGANIZATIONS

The naval station is a small base, only a few miles in each direction. Although amenities are limited, most Americans find that the base offers many of the comforts of home. There is a Commissary stocked with American brands of food. The Navy Exchange (NEX) sells American clothing, shoes, furniture, kitchen supplies, household goods, baby supplies, outdoor/yard equipment, and toys. The DoD school employs American teachers for Preschool through High School, and classes are taught in English. The Naval Hospital offers quality care for general practice, specialty clinics, and emergency needs. Like most military bases, there is a Fitness Center, a Chapel offering a variety of religious services and programs, a Library stocked with books in English (and some in Spanish), a Child Development Center, and restaurants (including Starbucks, Subway, KFC, and Taco Bell). There is also a U.S. Post Office, Laundromat, Dry Cleaner, Barber, Beauty Shop, Golf Course, Bowling Center, Movie Theater (indoor and outdoor), and Navy Federal Credit Union to assist with all your needs. Numerous other services and organizations offer volunteer opportunities, social membership, classes for youth and adults, or travel events. Of course, if you cannot find a particular item or club on base, you are also able to look in the surrounding Spanish towns. Local soccer clubs, swim teams, dance studios, and running clubs are all used to receiving American members. So there is plenty to do on base, for those who choose to get involved. Representatives from many of the following services will be present during the ICR class to explain their programs and answer questions. The following list is not comprehensive, but it highlights some of the services that are unique to Naval Station Rota, and explains ways this duty station differs slightly from other military bases.

AUTOPORT: The base gas station sells gas in dollars and gallons, typically for a price much lower than what you would get at European gas stations. You can also apply for a Cepsa card to get gas at a reduced rate at Cepsa (gas) stations throughout Spain. The Autoport conducts annual inspections (ITV) required by Spanish law. The repair shop can handle oil changes, and some repairs of either American or European vehicles, but usually replacement parts and tires are special ordered when needed, and delivered to base when available. For most repairs and body work, you will be directed to a Spanish shop off-base, where the work is typically very affordable. However, if your car is under an American warranty, check with your provider where service can be received.

BANKING: Navy Federal Credit Union is the only American bank on base. You may keep your other American banking accounts open and access them online, but you will pay fees at the ATM machines on base. In addition, make sure you are familiar with your American bank's process for remotely depositing checks. Some will allow them to be scanned from your phone, while other banks require checks be mailed directly to them, in which case it would take weeks for you to have access to the funds. You can cash checks on base at the Navy Exchange (NEX), or at the PSD (Personnel Support Detachment) office in Building 1. If you choose to open an account with Navy Fed, they have low fees and minimum balances on their checking and savings accounts, and will not charge you at their four ATM's on base. There are also two Spanish bank located on base: Banco Popular and Banco BBVA. It will be necessary to open an account with them if you rent a property off base, use utilities off base, attend a Spanish school, or purchase a Spanish cell phone with a monthly fee.

BEACH: There is one beach on base, called Admiral's Beach. It is located next to the port. The beach is owned by the Spanish and sometimes used for Spanish military training. However, as long as it is not being used for training purposes, it is open to families with base access. Entrance is possible year-round, whenever the gates are unlocked. During the summer, there are showers, restrooms, and a snack cart. There is no cost to visit the beach. This is one of the only beaches in the area that is NOT a topless beach.

CHAPEL: There is only one base chapel, so it offers a variety of services in English for many religious denominations, to include Catholic, Protestant, Jewish, and Latter Day Saints. There are services every weekend, activities offered throughout the week—including Bible Studies, prayer groups, children's church—and Vacation Bible School during the summer. The base has a staff of several Navy chaplains from different denominations, and a staff of religious program specialists (RP's) to assist with activities. There is an on-site nursery with child care available during most services.

Some active groups affiliated with the chapel include the Protestant Women of the Chapel (PWOC), who meet one morning each week for fellowship and scripture study and provide child care for free during their meetings. The Catholic Women's Group (CWG) also meets for prayer and study. There is a group for Mothers of Preschoolers (MOPS), which is a national Christian organization, to support mothers of young children in their vocation as mothers.

For contact information and details about Religious Programs, see the CNIC website's Installation Guide:

http://www.cnic.navy.mil/regions/cnreurafswa/insta llations/ns_rota/about/installation_ guide/religious_programs.html.

CHILD DEVELOPMENT CENTER (CDC): The CDC on base operates similarly to CDC's at any other military installations in the States. Care is available for children ages 6 weeks-5 years of age. Full-time care is from 6:30am-5:30pm, with priority given to families with dual working spouses or single military personnel. Rates are based on total family income. Hourly care is available at a flat hourly rate on a first-come basis, with reservations possible up to 30 days in advance. Evening hours are only available once a month. To receive care, your child must first be registered at the CDC. You can pick up an application packet in person, or apply in advance online through the MWR website under Child and Youth Programs. Presentation of the child's updated shot record, and parents' current Leave and Earnings Statement (LES) are required for full-time registration. For children with medical needs, such as the use of an inhaler or epi-pen, or children with food allergies, documentation from a doctor is needed before the child can begin receiving care in the center. You will need to register before your child can attend the CDC, even during ICR classes, so it is advisable to hand-carry copies of those documents with you when you move.

The CDC also offers a Spanish Immersion Preschool program for children ages 3-5. This is further discussed in the School section.

> The CDC Registration packet is available online. Visit their website to learn about childcare options, and how to enroll your children in the CDC while you attend ICR upon arrival:
>
> **http://www.rotamwr.com/activities/child-development-center**

COMMISSARY: Like most military bases, Rota has a commissary available to American military personnel and DoD family members. It is open 6 days a week (closed on Mondays), and sells all American products, in dollars, at cost plus a 5% surcharge as determined by the DoD regulations. The Commissary sells fresh produce which is purchased locally. Their fresh milk products are manufactured in Holland meeting FDA and USDA sanitation standards. Other dairy products that come from Denmark meet the required standards necessary to be sold at the commissary. They sell fresh U.S. meat which is cut and packaged out of the Central Meat Processing Plant in Germany and sent to the Rota Commissary for sale. You will be able to find all your favorite brands of seasonings, pasta, soups, frozen meals, beverages, and snacks. Always check expiration dates. The Commissary has a deli section that provides fresh-cut meats and cheeses, and a Bakery that makes pastries and fresh bread daily. You can special-order party items like decorated cakes, fruit and veggie platters, or sandwich trays. You can use American coupons up to 6 months past their expiration at the commissary. There is a Rewards Card program to use online coupons in addition to the traditional coupons and flyers that are available at the store. The commissary also accepts vouchers for individuals on the WIC (Women, Infants, and Children) program. Remember that baggers work for tips only.

In addition to the Commissary, there is a **Mini-Mart** open daily, with a small selection of groceries, dairy and frozen foods, as well as a full selection of beer, wine, and liquor. They also sell household goods like medicine, cleaning products, home décor, and school supplies.

EDIS (Educational and Development Interventional Services): EDIS offers a variety of services to families of children with developmental or psychological disabilities, including anyone registered with the Exceptional Family Member Program. The office offers free screenings for young children, and therapy for children who have speech or physical delays. Children can also be referred through the DoD school on base. There are playgroups for children and parents, and visits that can occur either at home or at the EDIS center. This is a great resource for any family who has concerns about their child and needs professional advice.

For information about referrals, and EDIS's screening and evaluations programs, visit their website:

http://www.med.navy.mil/sites/nhrota/ Patients/Pages/EDIS.aspx

---

FITNESS CENTER: The base fitness center is available for all military personnel, DoD employees, and families. It includes an indoor pool, outdoor track, multipurpose turf field, basketball court, and several weight and cardio machine rooms, as well as locker rooms and a sauna and Jacuzzi area. Group classes such as Zumba, spin, aerobics, and yoga are offered on a regular schedule, some for a low fee. Trainers can be hired to assist with personal goals. There are monthly activities and workout challenges, such as fun 5k runs, or an annual Duathlon or Sprint Triathlon. There is also a Family room in a converted handball court, where parents can bring their children to play on one half in a padded, toy-filled area, while the adults remain present and use the equipment on the other side of the room. There is no childcare available at the gym—only at the base CDC.

FLEET AND FAMILY SUPPORT CENTER: The FFSC conducts classes, events, and programs that are important to families stationed at Rota. The center has several full-time employees to assist with the ICR orientation seminars, WIC program, educational counseling, family counseling, sexual assault advocacy, and financial seminars. Classes such as Beginner Spanish, Resume Building, New Baby, or Dealing with Stress are offered on a regular basis. Cultural activities like cooking classes and presentations of Spanish customs are available seasonally. Each month, there is at least one day trip planned to a local town or event. These are very low-cost trips designed for families, and include a bus and a local tour guide. They are a great way to explore the local region.

HOSPITAL: Naval Hospital Rota is a beautiful facility located in the center of the base. It has about 250 medical professionals, and offers both inpatient and outpatient care, particularly in the areas of aviation medicine, internal medicine, dental, OB-GYN, optometry, orthopedics, pediatrics, psychiatry, family practice, physical therapy, and surgery. These services are available to active duty members and their dependents. The hospital also serves a large community of retired military personnel, as well as DoD families. At this base, Tri-Care covers all visits to the Naval Hospital, including the Emergency Room, Dentist (even braces!), and Optometrist. However, if you need to buy glasses or contacts you can take the prescription in town or order online and pay yourself. DoD civilians will be seen by the Dentist and Optometrist if space allows. It is usually very easy to make an appointment for a general check-up, since it is a small community. But there are a limited number of specialists for particular issues. If special needs arise that cannot be addressed at the Naval Hospital, you will be given a referral to see a specialist in the local area, and the hospital will provide a translator to attend appointments or procedures with you. There is an Exceptional Family Member Program (EFMP) and a screening process to assist any family with physical, mental, developmental, or learning disabilities. The overseas screening your family takes before being stationed here will help guarantee that any special needs can be met by the medical facilities available on base. Babies are born regularly at the base hospital, and will receive American birth certificates and passports. Occasionally, pregnancy complications require babies to be born at local Spanish hospitals, but families can still obtain an American birth certificate and passport for the child, which is done through the State Department as a recognition of a birth abroad.

The Hospital website includes a wealth of information:

**http://www.med.navy.mil/sites/nhrota/
Pages/Home.aspx.**

ITT, LIBERTY, AND OUTDOOR RECREATION:

ITT stands for Information, Tickets, and Tours. This program is offered through the base MWR Department, described on the next page. ITT provides a wide variety of activities and group travel programs. Some are daytrips to cities and events in the local area. Others are weekend-long trips throughout Europe offered during holiday weekends. Whether you want to learn more about the history of a Spanish town, attend a *fútbol* (soccer) match, go to a flamenco show or sherry tasting, participate in a 'foodie tour' with a local chef, or travel to Paris or Prague, ITT has something to interest everyone! Their trips can be more expensive than they would be if you planned it yourself, but ITT handles all the reservations, transportation, lodging, logistics, and local tour guides, so they can be a good deal for individuals.

Liberty offers similar trips, tickets, and tours, but their programs are planned and priced for single military personnel. Liberty also conducts regular events at the base movie theater and bowling alley.

The Outdoor Recreation Center plans numerous adventures trips each year, such as hiking, skydiving, surfing, snorkeling, snowboarding, and paintball. The center contains an indoor rock-climbing wall which can be rented for events. They rent out an assortment of equipment and outdoor tools such as tents, camping gear, sports equipment, GPS's, grills, bounce houses, and folding tables and chairs. They also have bicycles that can be rented by the day or by the week, which can be very useful when you first arrive.

MWR (Morale, Welfare, and Recreation): The MWR Department provides support through a wide variety of base programs and activities. They organize base-wide activities to celebrate holidays like Easter, the 4th of July, Halloween, and the Christmas Tree Lighting—all usually free to American families. They coordinate entertainment through Armed Forces Entertainment with visits from American celebrities like sports heroes, American Idol contestants, the Harlem Globetrotters, and the USO Sesame Street show. MWR runs the Child Development Center and School Age Care program (which is an after-school center for children age 5-9), as well as the Youth Center for children ages 10 and up. They also manage the Fitness Center, Aquatics Center, Golf Course, and Library, with regular activities ranging from exercise classes to golf tournaments to children's Story Time. Community classes are offered at various prices for children and adults. The schedule changes frequently depending on the skills of instructors in the community, but can include music, dance, or gymnastics lessons for children, Spanish language or fitness classes for adults, and hobby-related classes like photography or sewing. MWR manages the Pinz Bowling Alley, Flix Movie Theater, Drive-in Movie Theater, and the base restaurants Pizza Villa and Baskin Robbins, and the restaurant in La Plaza. MWR also manages the ITT, Liberty, and Outdoor Recreation programs. Their many field trip and travel opportunities are described previously.

> All of MWR's activities are published in the monthly magazine *Vamos!* which is available for free at many base locations. You can find out more on their website:
> navy/mwrrota.com
> **www.rotamwr.com**.

NEWSPAPER—*The Coastline* : Naval Station Rota has a weekly newspaper called *The Coastline*. It is published in English, and is a good source of articles covering events and changes that occur on the base. There are also articles about Spanish culture and history, or information about local towns. Submissions are accepted from volunteer writers, but most of the newspaper is written and published by a professional staff. There is a Classifieds section for selling cars, renting apartments, local jobs, etc. However, a broader selection of choices will be found through the Rota Yard Sales Facebook page.

If you are interested in reading Spanish newspapers, local papers include *Diario de Cádiz*, *Viva Jerez*, or *Europa Sur*. These are of course published in Spanish.

> *The Coastline* is available in print at numerous base locations, and can also be found online:
>
> **http://issuu.com/navstarota.**

POOLS: There is an indoor pool which is part of the base fitness center, open year-round, and used primarily for lap swimming and aquatic fitness classes. There are hours for open swim, but children will need to wear life jackets since there is no shallow area. The outdoor swimming pool is located in the Las Palmeras area of base housing, and is referred to as the Housing Pool. The Housing Pool is only open during the summer months—Memorial Day until Labor Day. It has several diving boards and water slides, a climbing wall, and offers Swim Lessons for a variety of ages, as well as designated lap swim times for adults. Most of the pool is at least 4 feet deep, but there is a separate shallow baby pool for non-swimmers. There is a fee to use the Housing Pool. Individuals can pay each day they visit, or families can purchase a season pass with prices based on the number of family members. There is a separate swimming pool located near the Spanish barracks, which is for Spanish families. Americans can attend this pool for free, with an invitation from a Spanish friend. The entire pool is over 5 feet deep.

RAWL: The Rota Animal Welfare League (RAWL) shelter is an on-base animal shelter and rescue program, run entirely by volunteers and donations. Many of the animals are rescued strays, while some are pets of families in transition, looking for a foster family or a permanent home. RAWL encourages adoption of cats and dogs. If you adopt, be sure to make arrangements to bring your pet with you when you PCS. RAWL is not a veterinary clinic (Vet services are available at a separate location on base) and does not board pets when families travel.

SELF-HELP STORE: This building, located in the Las Palmeras area of base housing, is a useful resource whether you live on or off base. If you live on base, you can use Self-Help to borrow many outdoor tools for free, such as lawn mowers, trimmers, shovels, and rakes. They also loan tools that can be used inside, such as concrete drills and dehumidifiers. Self-Help provides free replacements for the air filters in base housing (which should be changed monthly) and replacement burner pans for the stove. They also loan out cots that can be used when you hosts guests in base housing. The cots are single, but I find that putting two cots together with a double or queen air mattress on top makes a comfortable bed for visitors! If you live off base, you can get transformers, fire alarms, and carbon monoxide detectors for your home from Self-Help.

THRIFT STORE: The Navy Marine Corps Relief Society runs a thrift shop on base. They accept donations of children and adult clothing, furniture, household items, and baby gear, which are all sold at reasonable rates. The thrift shop is located next to the NCTAMS telephone office on base, and is run by volunteers. Donations can be accepted any time, if left in their outdoor donation bin. Shopping can be done any time they are open, which is usually several days each week, and Saturday mornings. The shop is available to all American and Spanish military and DoD families.

TRANSPORTATION: Rota has a no-fee shuttle bus service provided by the Public Works Department. The bus makes a circuit throughout the base with stops at designated locations including the base housing areas. All U.S. I.D. cardholders may ride the bus. Check the on-base schedule to find out what time the bus begins and ends for the day.
There is also a taxi stand in front of the NEX, with taxis prepared to take you around base, or into Rota or Puerto. Taxi fees are based on the meter and distance of travel.

U.S. POST OFFICE: This is available to handle all of your shipping and receiving needs. All military and civilian personnel assigned to Rota will have an FPO AE address through their command. This functions as a US address, so families in the States can send mail and packages to an FPO address and pay standard domestic shipping rates. You can determine this address before you move, since mail is sent to your command, not to your actual house, whether you live on or off base. Conversely, personnel stationed here pay domestic rates to ship things back through the States. The Post Office cannot be used to ship anything from which you will receive a profit, so groups organizing fundraisers, or individuals with home businesses, will have to respect specific guidelines and potentially use the Spanish Post Office instead. Additionally, eBay and similar auction sites cannot be used to sell products while stationed here. But most online purchases from major brands like Amazon, Wal-Mart, and Target will ship to FPO addresses, as long as the product meets size and weight requirements, and does not contain liquids. It is easy to order and receive American products through the base Post Office. Just remind family members not to write the word "Spain" anywhere on the package, or else it will be routed through Madrid and potentially lost or delayed.

WELCOME TO ROTA CENTER: There is currently an office located just outside the Rota gate, in the town of Rota, which is a cooperative effort between the base and the Rota Tourism office. Bilingual local residents are there to answer any questions Americans have about travel, Spanish food, and where to go or find particular items. They run free tours of Rota weekly (usually on Tuesdays), where guests ride a tourist train around the city, stop at local stores and businesses, and enjoy free tapas for lunch at a Rota restaurant! The office hosts multiple cultural events throughout the year.

WIC (Women, Infants, and Children): This government program is available for American military and DoD families stationed at Rota. Just like in the States, families will qualify for assistance with certain grocery items based on income, family size, and children's ages. The qualification standards are calculated differently overseas, so some families who did not qualify in the States may be eligible here. WIC vouchers can be used on particular food items such as milk, juice, cereal, produce, cheese, eggs, and wheat bread. Of course, they are only accepted at the Commissary on base, and will not be accepted at any grocery store in town. The WIC office is located in the Community Support building, near the Fleet and Family Support Center offices.

TECHNOLOGY: PHONES, INTERNET, AND TELEVISION

Not all American electronics will work in Europe, but that doesn't mean you should leave them all at home when you move. Here's an explanation of what you need to buy new, and what will work automatically.

ELECTRIC OUTLETS

The shapes of electrical outlets vary throughout the world. In the United States, the two straight aligned bars on an electrical plug are standard, so everything you buy in a US store plugs into the wall of an American home. In most of Europe, including Spain, the standard shape is two ROUND aligned plugs. In order to fit an American plug into a Spanish outlet, you need to use a small adapter which has input for the American shape plug and output plugs to fit the Spanish outlet. These adapters are about $2 a piece, and available at the NEX on base, so it is fine to bring all your current small appliances: computers, printers, toasters, coffee makers, hair dryers, etc. On base, the houses have all been outfitted with American style outlets in the walls, and the electricity has been converted to 110 volts, so everything you bring will work precisely as it did in the States, and you will only need the adapters when you travel.

Off base, there is another important difference to be noted. Not only are the shape of Spanish outlets different from American plugs, but the electrical output is much different, too. Spain uses 220 volts of electricity as its standard. America uses only 110. So even if you adapt the shape of an American appliance to plug into a Spanish wall, the appliance will still fry from the high voltage, unless you use a transformer to step down the voltage and make it safe for your appliance. If you move into off-base housing, you will be issued two or three transformers from the Self Help store. To use an American appliance in a Spanish home, plug the appliance into the transformer, and the transformer into the wall. You will probably use just 1 transformer in the kitchen, and another in the living room, so some people find it tedious to constantly move it around and unplug everything. Some appliances like TV's, phone chargers, and computers automatically transition between 110 and 220 volts, but always read the back of the appliance first! If it is dual power, it will say 110v- 240v and 50-60 Hz. Small appliances like lamps, hair dryers, toasters, etc. usually do not transition automatically and would require the transformer. It can sometimes be cheaper on the energy bills to purchase Spanish small appliances (new or secondhand) and use them instead, and resell them before you move.

TELEPHONE INFORMATION

In Spain, you only pay for outgoing calls and texts, not for calls or texts received.

Spanish phones have 9-digit numbers. Most on base numbers are listed in 7 digits. This is called a DSN. To use a Spanish phone to call a DSN line on base, you cannot dial the 7-digit number. Instead you must dial 956-82-****. So if the extension is listed on base as 727-1111, then from a Spanish phone you would dial 956-82-1111.

To call a base number from the United States, you will have to first dial the international code (011), and Spain's country code, which is 34. Therefore, if a base number is listed as 727-1111, when calling from the United States, you would dial 011-34-956-82-1111.

The Emergency number for Fire, Ambulance, and Police in Spain is 112. On base, you can dial 911 to receive emergency services, or 727-2911, but in town you should call 112.

For a list of Rota's important phone numbers on base, visit the official Phone Directory, available through CNIC Rota's website:

http://www.cnic.navy.mil/regions/cnreurafswa/
installations/ns_rota/about/
installation_guide/
phone_directory.html.

This page has dialing instructions for base and from the States, and will be updated regularly to reflect accurate extensions and names of contacts.

CELL PHONES:

Most American cell phones will not work in Europe unless they are made for international use and have an unlocked SIM card. To get your American SIM card unlocked, talk to your phone provider before you leave the States. Your plan usually cannot be under military suspension when you make the unlock request. Your provider will send you a code, and once it is verified the card will be unlocked. You will not want to continue service with your American provider, even if they have international coverage, due to the high cost. While Verizon, Sprint, and T-Mobil might claim they have international coverage, none of those companies have stores here to provide long-term plans or service. It may be a good idea to get international coverage for the first few weeks here with your current provider, but you would not want to use that as a permanent option. Buying smart phones here can be very expensive, but the price for unlocking them varies. It is best to bring an unlocked smart phone, then buy a Spanish SIM card and begin a contract or a monthly payment plan through one of several Spanish cell phone companies, such as Movistar, Orange, or Vodaphone. (Movistar currently has the best reception and service on base). If necessary, you can also purchase smart phones and data devices here, as well as a Spanish SIM card. Spanish companies do not do 2-year service plans. Instead, you get a 1-year plan and make monthly payments towards the value of the phone. There is a phone center at the NEX where you can purchase phones, service, and cut SIM cards. You can also go to phone stores in town.

Please note: to purchase a smart phone here and begin a payment plan, you will need an N.I.E. number (explained in the vehicle section) and a Spanish bank account. This will take at least two to four weeks to get set up, so do not expect to be able to purchase a data cell phone immediately upon arrival. If you are purchasing a prepaid instead of a contract phone, you can do that without the N.I.E. number. You will just use your passport or yellow TEI card issued the day you arrive on base.

If you don't need a smart phone or data plan, you can purchase a cheap Spanish cell phone for about 20 Euros, and pay cash whenever you need to add minutes. This is a simple option with no contract and minimal cost, so you can use it as much or little as you like, and quit using it whenever you choose. You will not receive a monthly bill, and you can top off your minutes at kiosks located at numerous stores and even gas stations in town. Of course, it will be a very basic phone with no internet access and probably no camera capabilities.

Your Spanish cell phone will not work when you visit or return to the States, unless you have an American SIM card. Some phones have slots for two SIM cards, which is a great way to guarantee it will work in either country.

LAND LINES:

If you move into base housing, you can use any brand of landline phone. The base Movistar representative will enable the jacks in your home, and each house comes with a pre-assigned 7-digit DSN number. You can plug in any phone that you already own, and use it as your land line. For a flat monthly fee, those who live on base can dial other base DSN lines, as well as Spanish landlines and cell phones. To call a cell phone from the land line, you have to dial 18- first.

Off base, you will have to discuss land line options with your landlord. Some people find it easier to just use cell phones, but of course you can use the land line in your rented apartment or house and pay the monthly bill.

INTERNATIONAL CALLS:

Because of the high expense to call the United States and other countries from a Spanish phone, most people use either Vonage or Magic Jack to have an American phone number that can be used to dial or receive calls. Family in the States can dial the number for the same rates as they would be charged for any other American number. Vonage charges a flat monthly fee, and incoming calls are free. Magic Jack charges an annual fee of about $30. Vonage boxes will only be shipped to American addresses, so if you plan to use their service, you must order it before you move to Spain. Magic Jack is sold in the States or at the NEX on base, for about $60.

You can also use programs like Skype or Facetime to make free phone or video calls through a computer or Apple device. The person you are trying to reach must also have the program installed.

INTERNET

Whether you live on or off base, you can use a Movistar modem for Internet access. These can be obtained through the NCTAMS office on base, and set up for a standard installation rate. The flat monthly rate is paid to the base phone office, and includes an equipment rental fee that cannot be avoided, even if you use your own router. The internet speeds are average, and adequate for most downloads and streaming shows.

In town, some areas have the option for faster Internet speeds with providers like Ono, Vodaphone, Orange, Axartel, or Gartel. Monthly fees will be charged based on speed. You can shop around for the provider that serves your area and suits your needs.

The only drawback is that a Spanish modem (on or off base) provides a Spanish IP address. If you subscribe to American companies such as Netflix, Amazon Prime, or Hulu+, your access to their sites will be blocked when you sign on with a computer using a Spanish IP address. The way around this is to use a VPN-blocking program such as Strong VPN, UNblockus.com, or Hola. These programs allow you to turn your Spanish VPN address off, and temporarily use an American IP address for any computer, laptop, PlayStation, Xbox, Wii, etc. They all have slightly different abilities and costs, so choose one that will work for you. Some companies require you to buy a particular modem, others will work with an American modem you bring with you or purchase here at the NEX. Be advised that there are many illegal ways to change your VPN for free, but if you want to do it legally you should pay an annual fee for the service.

When ordering products online from American companies, you must first check if they will ship to FPO/AE addresses. Many companies like Amazon, Wal-Mart, and Target do, but have restrictions on product size or weight that can go through the USPS. Sometimes, if the FPO option does not appear in the drop down menu, you can select New York as the state, then write FPO/AE as the city. Military mail was formerly routed through New York, though it has recently been diverted to Chicago. It is recommended to contact the provider directly and confirm shipping possibilities if FPO is not an option.

TELEVISION

To watch TV shows online, you will need to change your IP address, or get a VPN blocker, as described on the previous page. If you have an Apple TV, you can change the IP address on the TV and then just purchase the shows you want. Another option is to purchase a Slingbox, which must be set up to a cable box in the United States (usually at a relative's house). It costs $250 for the equipment and set-up, but after that usage is free and you can watch American shows as they come out.

If you live in town, some houses are already equipped to receive Spanish cable TV services, which will provide about 100 channels at no cost. (Additional premium channels are available for monthly fees). Most shows, of course, are in Spanish, with the BBC and maybe one other channel playing shows in English. If the shows are movies or news originally broadcast in English, than many TV's can convert to the original language. But the cartoons and Spanish shows are a great way for families to learn the language. Also, you have to purchase a cable converter box for about $100 so that your American TV can receive the Spanish signal, or use a European or multi-system television. You may also pick up a converter box in the base self-help store to allow you to view AFN, (American Forces Network), in your off-base home. The housing office has a list of people who can install it for you. You pay an installation fee of about $100, which includes the satellite dish and the set up. The box can be used for the duration of your stay, so you can view the 12 AFN channels, which are all broadcast in English. Most American TV's can be used off base, as long as they are able to convert to the 220-volt power in Spanish plugs.

On base, the AFN cable is available for free, and all houses are wired to automatically receive only the American AFN signals. Base housing is pre-wired to receive AFN without a cable box, so a TV cable plugged into the wall will automatically pick up the AFN signal. There are no DVR options. You can request an antenna to receive Spanish TV signals, but you will need a converter box or a European TV to actually play the channels.

The American Forces Network (AFN) is American programming that is available worldwide for troops who are deployed to the Middle East, or stationed in Europe, Asia, or the Pacific. The good part is that you can watch TV in English, and for free, while you are stationed here. The drawback is that there are only a few channels. There is one news channel, which cycles all the major news shows-CNN, Fox News, NBC, etc. for one hour at a time. There is a movie channel, a family channel, and one called AFN Pacific which is time adjusted for people on the opposite side of the globe. There is at least one sports channel that plays some games live, and replays others, depending on the time difference. (To watch the Superbowl, for example, you can either stay up all night, or watch the replay the next day.) The top-rated American shows are played on a regular schedule, usually the day after they air in America, but many people use other services to view their favorite shows online. In general, the programming is designed to be popular for young men. One interesting aspect of AFN is that it is a non-profit government program, so there are no commercials. The commercial breaks are replaced with military infomercials.

AFN also operates a radio station that provides English programming and hit American songs 24 hours per day. Currently, their frequency is FM 102.5.

EMPLOYMENT

Many military spouses are eager to find employment when they arrive in Spain, but the job search can actually begin before you move. First, be aware that American citizens will not typically be allowed to seek employment off-base, regardless of their Spanish fluency, because they will not have a VISA allowing them to work in Spain. So your employment opportunities are limited to the base itself. Next, it is important to note that the Agreement on Defense Cooperation that allows Americans to work here contains specific requirements about employment on base. The base is required to employ a 70% Spanish national workforce at all times. That means only 30% of the jobs are available to American citizens, so postings are filled quickly, and employment is very competitive. Most positions are full-time, but there are also part-time opportunities. Most civilian jobs that are available are through the NEX and Commissary (baggers and I.D. checkers), the base DoD school, the Child Development Center or with MWR. So finding a job that will further your career is often unlikely. Families should be aware of the employment situation before the move, so that they can plan accordingly.

Most jobs will be listed on the Naval Station Rota Human Resources website:

http://www.cnic.navy.mil/regions/cnreurafswa/installations/ns_rota/about/departments/human_resources_office.html.

MWR positions are posted on the MWR website:
http://www.rotamwr.com..

Jobs at the Navy Exchange are listed on their website:
http://www.NavyExchange.jobs.

WELCOME TO ROTA

TO APPLY FOR JOBS ON BASE …

Begin by contacting the Human Resources department's Employment Office at 727-1643 or 727-1635. See the links on the previous page for websites with job listings. Jobs are also posted in Building 1, and advertised in The Coastline newspaper. You may apply for a job on base up to 30 days before you arrive here. Applicants must be U.S. citizens and command sponsored to qualify. A resume or OF612, the applications for Federal Employment, need to be filled out and submitted for each job you are applying for. Applications may be submitted to Human Resources Monday through Friday from 8 a.m. - 4 p.m. MWR has their own administration office to handle their positions, so MWR jobs are not always listed with Human Resources.

The Fleet and Family Support Center can also help direct civilian spouses to employment opportunities. They offer resume writing classes, and can give personal direction to help you. They can be reached at 727-3232.

If you currently have a small business run from home, such as selling baked goods, crafts, or product lines like Pampered Chef or Mary Kay, you may still be able to continue your work when you move. You will have to contact the Region Legal Services Office, located in Building 1, to have your business 'base approved.' This means that you have paid the appropriate fees, filled out the registration forms, and agreed to adhere to specific regulations. For example, you cannot use the U.S. Post Office to purchase business items, so you will have to use the Spanish Post Office instead, or have someone in the States ship products to you. It can take a bit of time, but once completed, you will be able to sell your products here, and distribute them to your customers.

55

HOUSING OPTIONS

BASE HOUSING:

If you are interested in living on base, you can begin your housing application before you move here. Use the (Housing Early Application Tool (HEAT), which can be found at: http://www.cnic.navy.mil/ffr/housing/heat.html to get in touch with the Housing Office and let them know your interest. Wait times for base housing vary greatly depending on family size, number of families PCSing, and number of families arriving.

Even though base housing is located at one edge of base, many people bike, run, or ride a motorcycle/moped to work, since the commute is only a few miles. The Commissary, NEX, and most other services are centrally located, so they are all 1-2 miles from the housing area. The DoD school is located in the center of the housing area. There are numerous parks and playgrounds scattered throughout housing, and an outdoor swimming pool which is open during the summer months. There is also a base shuttle bus which runs through base housing to major points of interest on base during morning and afternoon work transit times.

For updated information on housing wait times, check-in procedure, and off-base estimated housing costs, visit the Rota Housing website:

**http://www.cnic.navy.mil/regions/cnreurafswa/
installations/
ns_rota/ffr/housing_and_lodging/
housing-quick-reference.html**

Base housing is available to all military families, but you will qualify for certain areas of housing based on rank and family size. All houses include a full kitchen, complete with stove/oven, dishwasher, refrigerator, freezer, and microwave provided by the housing office. Houses are also equipped with a laundry washer and dryer, as well as central heat and air conditioning. Water in Rota is safe to drink from the tap, and tests are conducted on base yearly to ensure water quality meets American as well as Spanish standards. (Water does not contain Fluoride, so you can either purchase bottled water with Fluoride added, or the base Dentist can prescribe Fluoride drops for your children.) Maintenance of the house, common spaces, and all appliances is overseen by the base housing office, and repairs are made at no cost to military personnel. However, you are responsible for the maintenance of your lawn and outdoor space. If you do not bring lawn equipment, you can borrow it for free from the Self Help office, or hire a maintenance company.

All base housing has tile floors throughout the house, and tile walls in the kitchen and bathroom areas. There are pre-mounted curtain rods and towel racks. You are not allowed to drill into the tile walls, but you can drill into the concrete walls in other areas of the house. So do not bring any shelves or mounting pieces for the bathroom or kitchen, but DO bring your own curtains and rugs, because you will want them. The housing comes with pre-installed rolling blinds called *persianas* so you do not need to bring any window shades or shutters.

There are two areas of base housing. Las Palmeras houses were originally built in the 1960's as duplex structures, but some are currently being renovated, so many are now spacious 3 or 4-bedroom houses, while others are still small 2-or 3-bedroom duplexes. All are single story concrete structures with fenced-in backyards. Las Palmeras is the location of the base school and housing pool, and is closer to most base locations.

Las Flores housing was built in the 1980's as 2-story townhouses. Most have 3 bedrooms and 2 bathrooms. The structures have seen some aging, and a rolling renovation schedule is planned for the next few years, so they are not available to new occupants.

Housing layouts are available in the Naval Station Rota Welcome Aboard packet, which is available online at: http://issuu.com/navstarota/docs/welcome_aboard_package_2013.

HOUSING OFF BASE:

Many Americans prefer to rent a house or apartment in town, on the local economy. If you choose to live off-base, you will receive an Overseas Housing Allowance to cover the cost of rent and utilities. This is calculated differently than BAH. You can begin your house search before you move by contacting the base Housing Office and asking for a list of their approved local realtors. There are numerous other realtors in the area, who have not made the Housing Office waiting list. Once you arrive, you will be provided temporary lodging for one month to allow you to find housing off-base. The Housing Office will conduct a briefing when you first arrive, lead you on house-hunting trips, and assist you in understanding lease agreements. Take the time to walk through potential neighborhoods and get to know the area before you make a choice. It is common for Spanish homes to have bars on the windows and be surrounded by high fences. These are not signs of a high crime neighborhood. Violent crime is low in Southern Spain, but petty theft is quite common, so objects left in unlocked cars or unsecured porches and yards are always at risk. The homes are quite beautiful, often with swimming pools or gardens, although in general yards are small. Be sure to ask practical questions about your landlord or potential property: how will it be heated in winter and cooled in summer? How does the water heater/solar panel/ butano bottle system work? How and where do you get butano refills? What are average monthly utility bills? What responsibilities will you, the tenant, have for landscaping or general upkeep? Where is the nearest grocery store or market? (usually within walking distance). Pets of all sizes are usually welcome in Spanish homes, but it is good to ask about pet policies.

To rent a home or set up a Spanish bank account or utilities, you will first need to acquire an N.I.E. This is an identification number used for foreigners, and can be acquired at the Security Office on base. You will need to first go to the Banco Popular with exact change (13.36 Euros in 2014). Banco Popular will give you a receipt. Then go to the base Security Office. Show them the receipt, your passport, your military I.D., and your Spanish I.D. card. The N.I.E. takes 2-4 weeks to receive, so apply for it as soon as you arrive.

THE TOWNS AROUND BASE

ROTA is a tiny sea-side fishing village with two main gorgeous beaches. The streets are very narrow and houses are typically small. Yards are almost non-existent, and parking is limited. This is considered a good area for young couples, because of the small quarters (mostly apartments and townhouses, rather than stand-alone homes) and the good nightlife. You can walk from the base into Rota, so there are plenty of American bars and nightclubs. During summer, the tourists are up every night, but in winter it is a quiet little town where everyone knows everyone else. It is only a few minutes' drive to the base gate. Americans have been here for 60 years, and Rota survives on our business, so even though most shopkeepers and restaurant owners don't speak much English, you will see Americans everywhere. The downtown square has a castle and cathedral from the 13th century, and hosts small celebrations throughout the year.

EL PUERTO DE SANTA MARIA is a much larger town, with multiple neighborhoods and housing areas, each with its own flavor. There are plenty of restaurants, bars, and large chain stores, including a shopping mall. There are multiple beaches, all very popular in the summer. This is considered a good choice for families, because the houses are typically larger, come with more yard space and parking, and often have swimming pools. Most neighborhoods in Puerto are about 15 minutes from the base gate. It is a popular area for Americans living off-base. Puerto is a great source of Spanish culture, with a bull ring, a Cathedral, and a castle from the 14th century. The town celebrates festivals and parades throughout the year, usually on a larger scale than Rota.

CHIPIONA is north of the Naval Base by about 20 minutes. It is more removed from the base's American influence, so has a very authentic Spanish farming village feel. In summer it is a busy seaside vacation town, and in winter it is a quiet community with orange trees lining the streets and donkeys braying in the fields. It also has a good shopping and restaurant area. The school buses for the on-base school still stop here in certain locations, and there is currently a thriving American community in Chipiona.

SHOULD I LIVE ON BASE OR IN TOWN?

Well, each has its advantages and downsides, so you will have to weigh your own family's priorities and determine how many sacrifices you are willing to make. The best thing to do is to wait until you arrive, explore different areas in person, and get a true sense of the neighborhood and the commute.

PROS AND CONS OF LIVING IN TOWN:

Living in town is the best way to become part of the culture. Your family will have more opportunities to learn and practice Spanish. The Spanish people are extremely welcoming, and many Americans have great relationships with their landlords. Living in town provides the opportunity to become involved in daily life: walking to the beach or the market, attending Spanish schools or social clubs, and making new friends. The military provides an overseas housing allowance (OHA) for anyone who lives off base, which covers monthly rent for most houses in this area, as long as you stay under your OHA threshold. There are houses with beach views, built-in swimming pools, and beautiful gardens maintained by the landlord, all a short commute from base.

The traditional style of housing in this area is a multi-level home, with a kitchen/dining/living space on the main floor, bedrooms upstairs, and a basement or bonus room downstairs. There are many variations, but the opportunity to live on multiple levels with additional rooms is a benefit for many families who find base housing dull, cramped, or inadequate.

Living in town and adopting a Spanish lifestyle also has a lot of challenges. Not only do you have to learn the language, but you also have to find your way around and navigate a new culture. At first, everything will take two or three more steps than you expect, and this can be frustrating or exhausting to a family. It will also mean changing a lot of routines. The Spanish are on a completely different daily schedule and eat their meals at much later times than Americans. They stay up much later, often until 1 am, even with children. Be aware that the beautiful beach views will be packed with tourists all summer, and the Spanish like to party loudly all night long. Conversely, 3-5 pm is siesta time.

Off base, utility bills are quite high, and can vary greatly from month to month, making it frustrating to budget. Some months, utility bills can be 200-400 Euros in off-base housing. Energy expenses are quite high in Europe, so you must be diligent about unplugging appliances and using devices sparingly. Dryers are a luxury in many homes, so clothes are often hung on the line to dry. I have already explained the minor inconvenience of transforming between Spanish electrical plugs and American appliances.

In Southern Spain, the climate is fairly mild, so central heating and air conditioning are not standard in most houses. You can find it in some of the more modern expensive rentals, but for the most part off-base housing is VERY cold in winter, and unpleasantly hot in summer. You can use space heaters and fireplaces, or fans, but you will not achieve the climate control that is available on base.

Spanish kitchens are not usually equipped with the large appliances that Americans are used to. The ovens and refrigerators are much smaller. The Spanish typically do their grocery shopping each day. Some Americans find this to be easy, while others find it frustrating. The Housing Office can provide full-sized 220v/ 60 Hz appliances such as washers, dryers, air conditioners, refrigerators, and freezers for the full tour for anyone living off base.

Off base, maintenance is handled by a landlord. Sometimes this works out fine, but often Americans get fed up with the *mañana* attitude the Spanish have about taking care of things 'tomorrow,' which rarely actually means tomorrow. Numerous holidays and a relaxed work attitude mean that Americans need to be very patient about maintenance. Sometimes Americans' ideas of maintenance 'problems' differ from what the Spanish landlords perceive of as their responsibility, so it can be a touchy subject and occasionally lead to lawsuits.

Finally, remember that base housing is always free. If you live off base, you are given an OHA calculated by rank, which covers your rent, and a utilities allowance, which can cover some or all of your utility bills. Just because your military OHA benefits change does not mean your Spanish landlord will adjust your rent. So if you decide to live in town, make sure you can afford your rent, and have a cushion for unexpected salary changes. With the uncertain budgets in the military, and the possible changes in housing allowances, it may be safer to live on base than to be locked into a rental contract in town.

PROS AND CONS OF LIVING ON BASE:

If you live on base, you can miss out on many of the cultural opportunities all around you. The base is a little pocket of America, where business is conducted in English, prices are charged in dollars, familiar food and products are available, and the majority of your neighbors are American. The base is fairly quiet and comfortable, and you can live as an American without adjusting to Spanish meal times and late hours. This can be a blessing, or a waste of your European experience, depending on your desires and priorities. Some families find a balance by frequently exploring the surrounding area and taking day trips on weekends, while living on base and enjoying the comfortable American routines during weekdays.

One big benefit of base housing is free utilities, including heat and air conditioning. On military bases, electricity and water are provided at no cost, without limitations. Climate control and laundry machines are a luxury in most of Europe. On base, you only pay one bill—for Phone/Internet (2014 rates $60 per month).

Another benefit to base housing is the large, full sized kitchen. It includes a regular oven and stove, a dishwasher, a fridge/freezer, and even an additional stand-alone freezer for larger families. If you want American conveniences, then you will be happier on base.

Base housing is maintenance free, maintained by the base, so you don't have to pay for or worry about repairs. Usually, a call to the housing office can get things fixed within a few days. You are allowed to paint, but you must first get approval through housing and re-paint in white before checking out. There is a Self Help office (available whether you live on or off base) which will lend out tools needed for basic home improvements, but any broken appliances or leaks will be handled by the housing repair office for free.

If you live on base, housing is free. You will not receive OHA or a utilities allowance while living on base. You will still receive COLA (Cost of Living Allowance) to accommodate for the exchange rates between the Dollar and the Euro. COLA is rank and dependent specific.

HOSTING GUESTS ON BASE

Whether you live on or off base, you have the ability to host family members or unrelated guests on base. You should apply for a pass before your guests arrive in Spain, because the process takes several days, and they will need a valid pass to get through the gate. If your guests will be staying with you in base housing (which is permitted for up to 30 days for up to 4 family members at a time), you must fill out a form at the base Housing Office, and wait a day or so for approval from the housing director. Note that the military sponsor must sign the form. Then bring that to the Security Office, along with the full legal name and passport or driver's license number of each guest. Fill out the white form with this information. Again, it must be signed by the military member. If you want your family members to be able to enter the NEX or Commissary, check off the box on the form. It will take at least one day to be approved by the Security office. Once approved, you will receive a white pass for each guest, and a pink pass to grant access to the NEX and Commissary.

Take note that even though family members with a pink pass can enter the NEX or Commissary with you, they cannot make purchases. A military I.D. is still required to make a purchase. Non-related guests cannot accompany you into the NEX or Commissary.

You may hire Spanish nationals to come on base and work for you (typically for babysitting, cleaning, or gardening work). To do this legally, you must secure a base pass for them to enter on certain dates and times. You must also go to the office in their hometown and register with the Spanish Social Security, so that they can be taxed.

For details explaining who has access to base, and a complete list of procedures for hosting Spanish nationals and other situations, please see the CNIC website on Visitor Information:

http://www.cnic.navy.mil/regions/
cnreurafswa/
installations/ns_rota/about/
installation_guide/
visitor_information.html.

CONCRETE WALLS

It is typical to find houses with interior and exterior concrete walls, both on base and in town. Drywall is not as common. So when you start to get settled, you may be stumped on how to hang items like pictures, shelves, TV's, or mirrors in your new home. There are several solutions. For heavier items, like shelves or flower pots, you will need to use a special concrete drill, or a hammer drill with a concrete bit, to drill into the walls. These are available at the base Self-Help building, located in base housing and described in the Base Services section of this chapter. For smaller items like pictures, you can use either the 3M hooks with removable adhesive on the back (available in several sizes and styles at the NEX) or you can use the Spanish hardware called *cuelga bien*. These are small plastic hooks with thin metal nails in the center. You can easily hammer it into the wall with a few taps, and hang pictures weighing up to several kilos. Weight limits are marked on each box. These can be found at Bricor in Jerez or local hardware stores.

SCHOOL OPPORTUNITIES

ON BASE:

Like most bases, Naval Station Rota has a DoD school on base with certified American teachers, and classes taught in English. The school, David Glasgow Farragut, has classes for Kindergarten-High School students, as well as a Sure Start program for 4 year olds. Enrollment is available for any military or DoD dependents. Tuition is free to military dependents, but there will may be a charge for DoD families. Whether you live on or off base, bus routes may be available. DoD education standards are followed, and students will take standardized tests that are offered in any other American public school. The only slight difference to an American school is that Spanish culture classes are offered once a week for all grade levels, and Spanish language lessons are taught every day. A variety of athletic activities and clubs are available for students of different ages and interests. To apply, you will need your military orders or DoD form 803 showing family members that are command-sponsored. You will also need the sponsor's military I.D., command address, child's birth certificate, updated shot records, and current records or transcripts from their previous school. To learn more about the school or the enrollment process, contact the School Liaison Officer.

For children ages 3-5, there is a Spanish Immersion program offered at the base CDC (Child Development Center) in the mornings. This is a class for American students, and adheres to DoD and CDC standards for curriculum goals. The teachers are native Spaniards and speak to the children in a mixture of both languages, so they become comfortable with the language and learn basic vocabulary. Tuition at the CDC is charged based on rank and LES.

Information about the base Elementary School is available at their website:
http://www.rota-es.eu.dodea.edu/.

The Middle and High Schools, which are located in the same complex, have their own website:
http://www.rota-hs.eu.dodea.edu/.

OFF BASE:

American families are also allowed to attend local Spanish schools, and here there are a variety of choices. Spanish public schools will accept American students if they have space in their classrooms. Children age 3 and up are eligible to attend Spanish public school full-time. Enrollment is free, and you pay only a small annual fee that covers the cost of books and supplies. There is a 'lottery' process that begins in March for the upcoming school year. While you can make a wish list of schools you prefer to attend, ultimately you will be assigned a school based on geographic location and availability. If you live off base, your children are eligible to attend school anywhere in their town. If you live on base, there is a dividing line for base housing to attend either Rota or Puerto schools. Americans must register the student at the town hall, and complete application forms (in Spanish) to submit to the school. School administrators typically speak only Spanish, and classroom teachers will typically not know any English, so parents wishing to enroll in Spanish schools should have a certain ability to speak Spanish, or have a friend to help them translate through the process. Public schools in Spain still teach religion (Catholic), although you can opt out of this if you choose. To learn more about the Spanish school enrollment process, contact the School Liaison Officer. They can provide the applications, and help you translate the initial forms.

There are also Spanish private schools, as well as *guadarias*— daycare centers. These charge monthly tuitions that vary greatly. Private schools are sometimes sponsored by churches, private organizations, or occasionally by the government. Most teach Catholic religion, and offer some opportunities that are not available in public schools, like bi-lingual classroom instruction, or additional extracurricular activities. Private schools offer a little more flexibility with schedule, allowing you to pick up a child early or drop off late, for doctor appointments or other reasons. At public schools, the gates are locked throughout the day, so drop off and pick up can only occur at specific times.

Spanish school days typically run from 9am-2 pm, at which point children return home for lunch and siesta. Drop off and pick up is only possible at those times, because afterwards the school gates will be locked. Lunch is not usually served at school, but there is a snack period, so most American families simply pack a lunch that can be eaten during snack time. Spanish children begin full-day school at age 3. Before that they attend *guardarias*, which are more like daycares with hourly rates. Teachers and most classmates will of course speak Spanish, though often there will be at least 1 other American student in the class. American children typically learn Spanish very quickly and easily, especially at a young age. The first month is a difficult transition. Some families love the opportunity to attend Spanish school and learn the language (for free!). Learning another language at any age can enhance brain development and improve numerous educational areas. Other families report dissatisfaction with the student's adjustment, the way Americans are treated in the classroom, or the general standards of Spanish education.

Spanish schools differ from American schools in a few key areas. First, of course the holiday schedule is based only on Spanish national holidays, which do not always align with American holidays. Secondly, the student to teacher ratio is much higher, (typically only 1 teacher, with no assistant, for a class of up to 30 kids) so even younger children will not receive personal attention or assistance with anything. Next, the educational material for each grade level does not compare precisely to American standard schedules, so when transferring from a Spanish school back to an American school, a student may or may not need tutoring to be caught up to other classmates. This becomes more of an issue in older grades. Finally, Spanish students are typically more physical and play rougher than is allowed at American schools. This is partly a cultural difference in the value of kids working out their own problems, but there are also occasional examples of Americans being picked on or targeted because they are different from all their classmates. So no one can tell you whether or not Spanish school will be best for your child. Some people have wonderful experiences; others have a terrible one. Do the research, ask questions, and make the decision for yourself based on your own child's needs and priorities.

HIGHER LEVEL EDUCATION:

This is an excellent duty station for adults to complete higher level education and earn a degree. Through the Navy College Office, military personnel, civilians, and dependents are able to earn a high school diploma equivalency through the GED exam, a vocational/technical certificate, or even a college degree. There are four accredited schools and universities represented on the base: Central Texas College, Embry-Riddle Aeronautical University, University of Maryland University College, and the University of Oklahoma. The four institutions of higher education are members of the Servicemembers Opportunity College, which can make it easier for students to complete degree requirements as they change duty stations. Most offer classes online, but there are some classes offered in person, as well. Keep in mind that certain degrees requiring hands-on labs or experience will be harder to take at this duty station. Financial assistance is currently available with Veterans Affairs (VA) education benefits or Navy Tuition Assistance. The Navy-Marine Corps Relief Society has initiated a Spousal Tuition Assistance Program (STAP) available only to military spouses overseas. For more information on this particular program, contact the Navy-Marine Corps Relief Society.

PART II:

SPANISH CULTURE

CLIMATE IN SOUTHERN SPAIN

The climate around Rota is very pleasant and mild for most of the year, often compared to Florida or Southern California. The spring and summers are gorgeous: sunny every day, with temperatures regularly in the 80's and 90's, but usually not much hotter than 100 degrees Fahrenheit. The sun is very strong, making skin cancer a concern. Sunglasses are essential most days year round. In the middle of summer, the afternoon heat is unbearable, which is why the whole country takes siesta. If you don't have air conditioning, you will shut your blinds and hide in the shade until the early evening, and you may have trouble sleeping at night without air conditioning or several fans. The summers are dry and cloudless for months at a time, making travel plans easy. A burn ban is usually in effect in base housing during the summer months.

The winters are damp and chilly. Temperatures hover around 40 degrees from December—February. It does not snow, but it rains often, and the combination of damp and wind makes it feel much colder than the thermometer reads. Rain coats, boots, and umbrellas are a must because the 'rainy season' lasts from November until March, and when it rains, it comes down in torrents. Winter coats, scarves, hats, and gloves are also important to bring, because even though it doesn't snow, it will be quite cold for several months each year. The architecture of Spanish buildings—tile floors, concrete walls, and clay roofs—is designed to keep you cool in the summer, but without central heat they are FREEZING in the winter. It is often colder inside the house than it is outside, because the sun cannot warm up the home's interior. So bring your slippers, robes, and blankets to be comfortable during the winter. The locals have a saying, *"Hasta el 40 de Mayo, no te quites el sayo."* It means, "Until May 40th (June 10th), don't leave home without your jacket."

Finally, since Rota is located on the coast, there are strong winds almost all the time. Hurricanes are not a concern on this side of the Atlantic, but there are frequent winds throughout the spring and fall, with occasional storms and gusts that can destroy fences, outdoor furniture, or outdoor toys. So keep trampolines weighed down with sand bags, and secure all lightweight furniture when not in use. Outdoor awnings can be used to provide shade, but should always be rolled up overnight so they will not be damaged.

LOCAL PESTS

Thankfully, there are relatively few poisonous creatures native to Southern Spain. There are no poisonous snakes in the area, and few household pests. Ants and anthills are plentiful, but can be handled with Raid or local pesticides. There are some spiders and scorpions that make their way into homes. (I have lived here two years and never seen a scorpion, but others have.)

The most dangerous pest is actually the *processionaria*, or processionary caterpillar. These caterpillars begin as eggs, which are typically found in pine tree areas. In spring, the eggs hatch and the caterpillars make their way down the trees and into the surrounding area. As they migrate, they form a line, with each caterpillar's head touching the tail of the one in front of it. It is a curious sight, and one that can attract attention from pets and children. Unfortunately, the caterpillars' defense mechanism is to shake tiny barbed hairs at their attackers when they feel threatened. The hairs have venom on them, which can be dangerous to adults, and is especially dangerous for children and animals because even one caterpillar's contact can cause painful swelling, skin irritation, difficulty swallowing, or vomiting. The barbs become airborne, and are especially dangerous if inhaled or ingested. They also leave some hairs behind as they move, so the ground and areas they have crawled over continue to be dangerous to pets and children, even after the caterpillars have moved away. So when you see these creatures, keep your distance! If one falls on you or gets caught in your clothing, you may need to visit the emergency room on base for treatment. Do not try to treat or control these pests yourself. Professional services are required to remove them, so if you have them at your house, contact your landlord or the housing office.

The base also has a problem with a large population of feral cats. These cats are wild, and have never been anyone's pet or lived in a house. They have a high chance of carrying diseases such as rabies. They should NOT be approached, handled, or fed. In the past, the base has tried to catch, neuter, and release them, but the process had no impact since many new cats are constantly attracted to the base. These cats are not the responsibility of the Rota Animal Welfare League (RAWL) and should not be approached. Please keep lids securely fastened on trash cans, as they will get into everything and keep returning to areas where they find food.

"SPANISH TIME" AND DAILY ROUTINES

The daily schedule for a Spanish person is usually quite different from that of an American. The Spanish eat, sleep, and work at different times than we do in the United States. The different routines are often one of the most challenging cultural adjustments for Americans living in Spain.

The Spanish start their day by waking up around 7 am and heading to work or school at 8 am. They usually do not eat much breakfast, only coffee. So around 9 am, it is typical to take a breakfast break to enjoy a *café con leche* and Spanish toast: fresh bread with jamón, cheese, tomatoes, or jam. It is almost like a breakfast sandwich. Eggs are not a typical breakfast food.

Stores usually open at 10 am, except on Sundays, when many stores are not open all day. Schools, stores, and businesses remain open until 2 pm, at which time adults and children return home for lunch and siesta. Spanish lunch is served around 2 or 3 pm, and is a large, hot meal: soup, stew, potato dishes, fillets of pork or chicken, or fried seafood. Most restaurants serve lunch starting at 1 pm, and then close around 4 pm. After lunch, most of the country takes a break (*siesta*) until around 5 pm. Stores and restaurants close, children go home from school, and some businesses close. This is essential in the summer, when—without air conditioning—it is too hot and uncomfortable to do anything besides hide inside in the afternoon, or go to the beach. Of course, not everyone can take a siesta, and essential services will remain open.

Around 5 pm, the country comes back to life: adults return to work, stores and businesses reopen until 8 pm (in winter, sometimes longer in summer), children participate in after-school activities. Although stores may have their evening hours posted as reopening at 5 or 6 pm, this doesn't mean the owner will return precisely on the hour. Stores reopen when the owner returns from siesta, so you may have to wait 15 or 20 minutes for a store to reopen, especially in the winter, when stores have more limited hours. Most people have a coffee or a 'snack' around this time, which for adults is usually *café con leche* and olives, but for young people is typically a *bocadillo*—a fresh roll of bread with some meat or cheese on it—or a bag of chips.

When the Spanish refer to doing something 'in the afternoon,' they typically mean between 5 and 9 pm. Americans refer to the afternoon as 1 pm until dinner time. But because the Spanish eat lunch later and then take siesta, they do their afternoon activities while Americans are preparing dinner.

Dinner for the Spanish is not usually served until 9 pm. Although there are some restaurants in Rota and Puerto that have 'American hours' and open for dinner at 6 or 7 pm, it is generally unusual to find restaurants open before 8 pm. At home, dinner is the lighter meal—often something cold or simple like soup, tortilla, or sandwiches. In restaurants, entrees can be anything from fried fish to grilled pork to steamed prawns, often served with fries. When going out for food and drinks, the Spanish will often begin with tapas (small appetizer portions) around 7 pm. It is common to go tapas-hopping to several restaurants in one night, stretching the meal into several hours, eating a small amount of food with each drink. See more about tapas in the Food section of Part III of this book. Even when going out for dinner at one restaurant, it is common for the meal to last until midnight. The Spanish typically stay up much later than Americans, often until 2 or 3 am on weekends. During the summer, the beach towns will be full of young vacationers who stay out until sunrise.

SPANISH CULTURAL DIFFERENCES FROM AMERICANS

When living in another country, Americans should expect to encounter continuous cultural differences from what is 'normal' or 'expected' in the United States. Some of these differences are anticipated, while others might take you by surprise. Every American reacts to Spanish culture differently, but it is helpful to remember that you, as an American, are the outsider. You cannot expect things to be done in Spain the way they are in your hometown in America. Sometimes things are different for understandable historical or religious reasons. Other times it is difficult to understand why things happen a certain way. Try your best to reserve judgment, and don't make cultural assumptions about the Spanish in general after just one encounter. The more you are willing to be accepting and adapt to change, the better you will be able to adjust to life in Spain. With that said, here are some of the cultural differences that usually stand out to Americans:

1. The lifestyle is very relaxed. Some Americans love this, but for most it is a change from our always-busy American lives. The Spanish take the time to enjoy life: they enjoy long, slow meals, they enjoy family time, they enjoy going for walks with their children. The flip side of this is that timeliness is not a Spanish trait. Stores and restaurants do not open promptly on the hour. Orders and repairs do not always happen on a prompt timeline. Guests often arrive 15 minutes after an announced time.

2. Family comes first. The Spanish are extremely family-oriented, often being born, growing up, and getting married in the same town. The younger generations take care of the older generations (or hire someone to care for them). Men are involved in family life, taking their children to the park and carrying them in public. Most holidays are celebrated with the entire extended family, in large gatherings with plenty of alcohol, music, and laughter. On Sundays, most stores are closed, because the Spanish spend the whole day with their families.

3. Work comes second. The Spanish work for a living, but do not live for working. The work ethic is very laid back, and family or fiestas can take precedence to work. Spain can be an extremely relaxing environment for Americans who are used to the constant rush and stress of the States. However, the *mañana* (tomorrow) attitude of procrastinating can also be very frustrating for people who are waiting for a store to open, for a vehicle to be repaired, or for a landlord to mend something in the home. Things do not always happen in a timely manner, and usually take longer than estimated. The laid back work attitude has also contributed to the economic crisis that has gripped the country for the last few years. Unemployment is currently around 25%, so those who have jobs are very interested in keeping them.

4. Life is a party. Or more accurately, one fiesta after another. There is almost always some kind of upcoming celebration to anticipate, whether it is one of the major annual events like Carnaval or Feria, a smaller local celebration like Andalusia Day, or a religious or culinary festival celebrated only in one town. Each town has their own schedule of fiestas, but they last most of the year, especially through the warmer weather from Easter until October. The Spanish take holidays and religious festivals seriously, so stores will be closed and people will be out in the streets for a parade or a fair near the town center. Americans usually have a 3-day weekend for holidays like Martin Luther King Day or President's Day, observing the holiday on the closest Monday. The Spanish celebrate holy days on the calendar date, even if it is a Wednesday or Thursday. So it can be difficult to keep track of all the holidays and business closings. But it is also fun to get out and enjoy some unique celebrations! Look for the holiday schedule at www.aytorota.es. It is explained in depth later in this chapter.

5. Restaurants are never open when you are hungry. Because the Spanish eat at such different times than Americans, it is difficult to find a place serving food around Noon or 6 pm. Restaurants don't open for lunch until 1 pm, then close at 4, and don't reopen until 8 pm! So you have to plan carefully, and maybe get a babysitter to go out for dinner.

6. Meals are leisurely. It is completely normal to spend 2-3 hours at a restaurant for a meal. Eating in a rush is an American trait. So the first few times you go out, you will probably be appalled at the lack of service and the difficulty in locating a waiter. It isn't bad service, it's just different standards. In America, we expect a waiter to check on the table frequently. In Spain, that is considered almost rude. Instead the priority is to leave the guest alone to relax and enjoy their meal. If you want something, including the check, make eye contact or wave your waiter over.

7. Alcohol is always available. Most Spanish drink frequently, and sometimes profusely. Beer and wine are available at every single public event, whether it is a sporting competition, a religious festival, or even a performance at your child's school. The legal drinking age is 18. Beer, wine, and sangria are the most common beverages, although hard liquor and mixed drinks are sold at all bars and similar establishments. The drunk driving limit is much lower in Spain: only 0.01 blood alcohol is permitted while driving a vehicle. So if you have even one drink in town, it is best to catch a ride with a taxi or friend, or have plans to walk home, rather than taking the risk of driving.

8. The Spanish adore children. If you have children, you will find it common for them to be greeted, touched, and cooed over in the streets with cries of *'Que guapo/guapa!'* (how cute!). Children are included in all festivals and celebrations, even those occurring in the middle of the night. Many large stores and shopping centers have play areas where children can be dropped off while you shop, or play while you eat. In restaurants and other public settings, children are often seen AND heard, unless it is a formal event.

9. Parking garages don't have cashiers at the exits. To avoid getting trapped at the exit gate, make sure you pay your ticket at the machine—*la cajero*—BEFORE you get into your car. The machines are usually located in stairways or near the exit. You pay while on foot, the machine validates your ticket, and then you have about 10 minutes to get in your car and drive out. Swipe the validated ticket at the exit, and the gate will raise automatically.

10. Spain is a Catholic country. Ever since the conquest of the Christian king and queen in the 15th century, the country has been exclusively Catholic. This means that every small town has its own church or cathedral, and almost all public holidays are rooted in some religious tradition honoring Jesus, Mary, or a saint. Public schools almost always teach Catholic religion as part of the curriculum, because there is no separation of Church and State like there is in America (although parents can opt out of these classes). There are public processions of statues on holy days, and national holidays from work for important Catholic feasts. Not everyone attends church, and you will not find a strict or moralistic Catholic attitude in the culture. Religion is simply part of the Spanish history and mindset. There are very few Protestant groups represented, as Spain endeavored to preserve pure Catholicism with events such as the Inquisition. There is however a growing presence of Islam, mainly in immigrant communities.

11. Andalusians (people living in Southern Spain) are extremely friendly and welcoming. The Southern United States is famous for its hospitality, and the same seems to be true in Southern Spain. People you barely know will offer to take you places, show you around, and invite you to cultural events. You will be invited to try new foods and drinks. Americans are sometimes surprised by this generosity and openness, and our natural reaction may be to decline the invitation and walk away quickly. Of course, use common sense and never go anywhere alone or with someone who makes you uncomfortable. But don't pass up great opportunities simply because they are offered with great zeal.

12. The sun stays up forever in the summer! Spain is in the wrong time zone. Currently, Spain is in the GMT+1 time zone, meaning it is in the same time zone as Italy and most of the Mediterranean—6 hours ahead of the East Coast of the United States. However, geographically, Spain is actually WEST of London. The time was changed during World War II, when dictator Francisco Franco sought to align Spain with the Nazis in Germany and Italy. It was never changed back. So in summer, the sun doesn't set until after 10pm.

13. Daylight Savings Time is still observed in Spain—spring forward one hour in March, fall back one hour in October. However, it is observed on a different date here than in America, usually a few weeks apart, so for a few weeks your family and friends in the States will be on a slightly different time than you.

14. The "first floor" is upstairs. In Spain, as in most of Europe, what we call the first floor is referred to as the ground floor, *planta baja.* When you walk upstairs to what they call the first floor—*primer piso*—you are on what Americans typically call the 2nd floor. So if you're looking for an office or apartment on the first floor, remember you'll have to go upstairs.

15. You will see a lot of skin. The Spanish concept of modesty is different from Americans. So, for example, all beaches in the area are topless beaches. It doesn't matter if women are young or old, thin or fat—they frequently go topless at the beach. The bottoms that are worn are usually thongs. Men typically wear tight bathing suits with a short cut, whether they are young or old. And young children are often completely naked, up until age 8.

16. Gender equality has not quite developed. While there are now more women in the workforce than in previous generations, household attitudes towards men's and women's roles have not changed much in the past hundred years. Cooking and cleaning are still almost exclusively women's work, as are most child-related tasks. Athleticism is a male-dominated field, but women are now becoming more involved in sporting events.

17. Europeans are much more energy-conscious than Americans. Spain makes excellent use of wind and solar power, yet energy costs are still much higher than in the States. Therefore, the Spanish are much better at conserving energy: central heat and air conditioning are not standard, many homes don't use dryers, and hot water is not always available for showers. You can open or close windows and blinds to control temperature, and you should unplug anything not in use. Recycling is common, but not mandatory, in most places off base.

18. Spanish plumbing is different. You will notice toilets are slightly different in a few ways. They use less water, so you will usually have an option to press one button for a partial flush (for liquids only) or a different button for a complete flush (for solids). In many public restrooms, it is typical to place toilet paper in a trash can instead of flushing it. Finally, many European toilets are designed with straight pipes instead of s-shaped pipes, so it can be common for sewage smells to come back out through toilets, sinks, or showers. This is a problem both on base and in town. Keep drains plugged when not in use.

19. Gardens are important. Even the smallest house or apartment will have flowers hanging on the walls, crammed onto tiny balconies, and growing in a narrow courtyard. The Spanish take a lot of pride in their homes and their gardens. There are even town competitions in the summer for the most beautiful patio. Houses and streets are generally neat and clean, so please do your part to keep it that way.

20. Girls always have pierced ears. The Spanish generally pierce a baby girl's ears just after birth, while she is still in the hospital. So a child without pierced ears is assumed to be a boy, even if she is dressed all in pink! (And even more interestingly, newborn boys are not usually circumcised, so asking for this at a Spanish hospital is seen as a somewhat cruel request.) If you want to get your daughter's ears pierced while stationed here, the safest place to go is the local *Farmacia* (Pharmacy) where they will use a sterile needle. You can also go to Claire's in El Paseo Mall, but there they will use a punch gun.

CALENDAR OF HOLIDAYS

There are TONS of local celebrations and festivals that occur throughout the year. Some are only celebrated in one town. Others are celebrated throughout Andalusia, or throughout Spain. The major holidays of the year are described below. National holidays are indicated, because schools, stores, and businesses will be closed on national holidays. Local holidays may be celebrated only in certain regions of Spain, or just in certain towns. Sometimes, if a holiday falls on a particular date and it happens to be a Tuesday or Thursday, the Spanish will have a 4-day weekend to celebrate the holiday. Other times, if the holiday date falls on a weekend, the school and business closings will be on the closest Monday.

> For more information about local celebrations, go to Rota's tourism page (in English): **http://www.turismorota.com/ENG_13/**.
>
> Or you can visit El Puerto de Santa Maria's page: **http://www.turismoelpuerto.com/**.

JANUARY 1: NEW YEAR'S (NATIONAL HOLIDAY)

Like many countries, Spain celebrates with a countdown and fireworks at the capital. The Puerto del Sol plaza in Madrid is the focus of the celebrations, and at midnight every eye turns to their clock tower. However, the Spanish have a unique tradition to celebrate the New Year. As the clock chimes midnight, people across the country attempt to eat 12 grapes, one on each chime, to bring them 12 months of luck the following year. It is an amusing and somewhat challenging practice, which the Spanish make easier by peeling and de-seeding their grapes ahead of time. The traditional drink is *cava*, which is like champagne. In Rota there is a big party with music in the Plaza d'España, but it all starts after the countdown.

JANUARY 6: THREE KINGS' DAY (NATIONAL HOLIDAY)

The feast of the three kings, also known as Epiphany, is on January 6. This is a huge celebration for Spanish families, because it is the day children receive their Christmas gifts. Christmas Day is usually a day to share a huge meal with family, but the gifts are exchanged on January 6. Spanish children do not celebrate Santa. Instead, it is the three kings from the Bible who brought gifts to baby Jesus that continue to bring gifts to Spanish children. In the weeks leading up to Three Kings' Day, figures dressed as one of the kings will appear at malls and town centers for photo opportunities. Children write letters to the three Kings, then a Royal Postman collects and delivers them by ship. On January 5, each local town has a Three Kings' parade, where the figures move through town on floats and throw candy to children. Correction: they pelt children with tons of candy. It can actually hurt! But the Spanish children love it, and it is a fun celebration. Depending on what day January 6 falls, the Spanish typically have several days off work for this holiday.

FEBRUARY 28: ANDALUSIA DAY

Andalusia Day is celebrated every February 28. It was this day in 1980 when the area of Southern Spain called Andalusia became an autonomous community of Spain. Schools and businesses are usually closed, and school children will do some cultural activities or events to prepare for the day. The Andalusian flag is two green stripes and one white horizontal stripe, so you will see this everywhere. Some local towns have parades or cultural events to mark the day.

CARNAVAL

The date for this celebration changes each year, because it is the week (or weeks) leading up to Ash Wednesday. Usually it is in late February or early March. In the United States, New Orleans is known for their Mardi Gras celebration. In Spain, Cádiz is the center of Carnaval activities. Carnaval is a riotous celebration of music, costumes, and of course food and drink. For a week or more, there are public and private celebrations in every town. Everyone dresses up in crazy costumes, similar to an adult Halloween party. There are parades, comedic musical performances, food tastings, and costume competitions. Transportation like busses and ferries run all night long to transport drunken revelers to and from the events. It is not a particularly child-friendly event, and in Cádiz especially there are huge pressing crowds. But there are smaller parades and celebrations in all the local towns, so you don't have to go to Cádiz to join in some great fun. Rota and Puerto both have small celebrations, and Chipiona's is particularly well-known and family-friendly.

SEMANA SANTA
(THURSDAY AND FRIDAY ARE NATIONAL HOLIDAYS)

The opposite of Carnaval, this is the somber celebration of the Holy Week before Easter. Again, the date changes each year, depending on Easter, but is usually in April. The celebration begins on Palm Sunday (the week before Easter) with parades that go from the churches throughout the town. On Holy Thursday and Good Friday, there are solemn, silent processions that begin and end at the church. During these processions, groups of men called brotherhoods carry enormous platforms on their shoulders, bearing the weight of the church's treasured statures of Jesus and Mary. It is a huge honor to carry the platforms, and brotherhoods train together for the event. The penitents wear tall pointed caps, which to Americans look like the Ku Klux Klan outfit. However, in Spain, they date to the Inquisition period, and designate someone who is doing penance to earn forgiveness for his or her sins. Crowds from the town will turn out for these processions and carry candles. Children collect balls of wax from the candles as souvenirs. Schools are closed all week, and businesses are closed Thursday and Friday.

APRIL RUNNING OF THE BULLS

The most famous festival with a running of the bulls is San Fermines in Pamplona, in Northern Spain, and occurs in July. This is what Hemingway wrote about in his novel *The Sun Also Rises*. However, there are still a few places in Andalusia that will host a smaller event. Arcos and Vejer de la Frontera have a running of the bulls every April. At least one large bull is released into the street, to thunder past the crowds of spectators. Men who attempt to outrun the bull usually wear white clothes and a red sash. However, military personnel are not allowed to participate in the running. They may only be spectators. Not all Spanish people support the activity, or bull fights. It is an old tradition, but modern Spaniards have very divided feelings about these events.

FERIA

Right after Easter, cities throughout the south of Spain (Andalusia) host a week-long celebration called *Feria*, which is often translated as 'Spring Fair.' Any good Spanish celebration involves drinking and music, and Feria is the ultimate festival: carnival rides, food, music, dancing, all-night drinking, horse shows, and fancy dresses. What's not to love?! The first Feria is traditionally in Sevilla, the regional capital, in April. After that, each city has their own week-long celebration. So Feria season actually stretches from April until October. Spanish don't always go to Ferias in other towns, but during the week it is in their town, they celebrate until dawn, and the Monday after Feria is often a holiday for a "recovery day."

The tradition of Feria began in 1847, in Sevilla. It was originally a livestock and agricultural event. But in typical Spanish tradition, they turned business into a party, and it became a popular annual event. While Feria is no longer an agricultural fair, horses still play an important role in the celebrations. The Andalusian horses that are bred in this region are famous for their graceful form and elaborate training. In Sevilla, horse-drawn carriages still bring the wealthy to the Feria grounds. In Jerez (the center of the breeding and training activities) it is called the Feria de Caballos, and presents horse shows and carriage rides for Feria attendees.

Feria attire: The Spanish love to dress up for Feria, particularly the women. The bright, ruffled dresses are the traditional dress, not only for Flamenco dancing, but for any Feria event. Most dresses feature polka dots and bright colors, although there are more 'modern' designs with stripes or other patterns. But... mostly polka dots. Spanish women have their dresses tailored each year so that they are perfectly form-fitting. Or they buy a new dress each year, depending on budget. New dresses cost from 100-400 Euros, but you can get them used at a discounted rate. The traditional attire for men is related to the 'cowboy' garb of the 1800's: dark pants, sometimes with spurs, a vest, a white shirt, and a flat, black, wide-brimmed hat, but you usually only see performers wear this outfit. Women take great care to coordinate their accessories, which include a shawl, a flower in the hair, sometimes a large comb in the hair, and of course the shoes. It is also common to see siblings or families with coordinated dresses. Wearing these dresses, women will break into the traditional *Sevillanas* dance. This is a beautiful dance with set steps and hand motions. Children often learn it in school, and classes for adults are offered on base and throughout the area. It is worthwhile to learn how to dance *Sevillanas* so that you can fully participate in the Feria activities. But if you don't dance, you can still enjoy the rides, games, food, and people-watching!

During the Spanish Civil War, Feria was supposed to be cancelled, but the Sevillians held it anyway, in defiance. During the 1920's it evolved into the gaudy, carnival atmosphere that you see today. Each city has its own Feria ground, which is a dirt area that is primarily used during this one week of the year. The entrance to the Feria is constructed anew each year, and is an elaborate gate, modeled off the entrance to the Feria in Sevilla. Over the Feria grounds, hundreds of lights hang in decorative arches. At night, they are lit up in many colors, adding to the festive atmosphere. Once you enter the Feria grounds, the area is lined with '*casetas*,' which in some cities are temporary tents, and in others are permanent buildings. The *casetas* are another product of the original agricultural fair. Tents were thrown up to provide shade for business transactions, and allow farmers to get a drink or something to eat. Now, each *caseta* is a complete restaurant, with a kitchen, bar, and dance floor. Each *caseta* is owned and operated by a different family, fraternity, or brotherhood, and the semi-private parties there continue overnight into the morning. Typical dishes available in the *casetas* are: fried squid, fried peppers, tortilla, jamón, and cheese.

Once you pass the dirt Feria grounds, there is another part of the Feria celebration that is basically a carnival. There are rides such as Ferris wheels, carousels, and bumper cars. Each ride has its own ticket stand, so there are few lines. The rides are surprisingly long, lasting up to 5 minutes. But they should be, since each ride is 3 Euros, per person! Thursday is Family Day at most Ferias, and the rides are half price. There are typical carnival games and food. Spanish fair food consists of hamburgers and chicken nuggets, falafel sandwiches, cotton candy, ice cream, and lots of donut stands. There are carnival games with prizes like stuffed animals, large balloons, etc.

Whether you go during the day with children, or at night with friends, Feria is a wonderful event for the whole family to enjoy. There are plenty of babies in strollers and young children there to enjoy the rides, as well as groups of teens hanging out together, and parents dancing and singing into the wee hours of the morning.

MAY 1: LABOR DAY (NATIONAL HOLIDAY)

May 1st is the Labor Day holiday, and is a holiday throughout the country. Stores and businesses will be closed, and most Spanish will spend the day with families.

EL ROCIO

Every year, the week before Pentecost (usually late May), about 1 million people from all over Andalusia gather in the town of El Rocio to celebrate *Nuestra Senora del Rocio*, Our Lady of the Dew. The pilgrims, or *Romeros*, have been making this journey annually since the 17th century. It takes four days or more to travel across Andalusia, because they ride on horses and pull colorfully-decorated wagons to carry their supplies as they camp and make their way towards El Rocio.

The tradition of Our Lady of El Rocio goes back to the 13th century, when a hunter found a statue of the Virgin in a densely wooded area of the modern-day Doñana Park, and built her a chapel on that site. On the night of Pentecost, the town of El Rocio has a huge celebration and procession of the statue of Mary, carrying her from the chapel of one brotherhood to the next. Devotion was originally a local event, but in the 17th century, other cities began to form groups, or brotherhoods, to make the pilgrimage together. Now, each town in this region sends their own brotherhood. The groups travel together riding horses, wearing traditional attire: short *traje* jackets and wide-brimmed hats for the men, and colorful ruffled feria dresses for the women. They are followed by wagons and modern caravan homes, which they sometimes camp in overnight, Some groups have large tractors pulling trailers of supplies. One essential supply is... wine! There are huge plastic barrels of manzanilla wine to fortify the Romeros on their journey. This is a joyful event. During the day, they pray and sing songs. At night, they make campfires, drink, pray, and sing. The pilgrimage is a family affair, with children riding in the wagons and caravans.

There are several routes the pilgrims can take, but they all eventually come to the Doñana National Park, which is a protected wildlife area. People are not allowed to travel though this park unaccompanied, so the Rocio pilgrimage involves lots of police watching the route and protecting against forest fires. To reach the Doñana Park, the pilgrims must cross the Guadalquivir river, so they all come together at the town of Sanlúcar de Barrameda to board ferries and enter the park. For two days, brotherhoods line up at designated times to board the ferry together. If you go, you will enjoy the festive atmosphere, with locals filling the riverfront restaurants and singing in the streets.

ALL SUMMER: BULLFIGHT SEASON

The Spanish tradition of bullfighting began in the 1700's, when nobles mounted on horseback would train by hunting bulls. The sport became very popular, and bullrings were constructed in towns throughout Spain. The bullring in Ronda is the country's oldest, and the one in Madrid is the country's largest. Bullfighting continues to be popular throughout Andalusia and in some other parts of Spain. During the summer months, you can attend a bullfight at the rings in El Puerto de Santa Maria, Sanlúcar de Barremeda, Ronda, or Sevilla. Each fight features three different matadors of varying skill levels, each usually fighting two bulls. Some have become so popular that they have achieved celebrity status in Spain. You can purchase tickets either for the *sol* (sunny) or *sombre* (shaded) side of the arena. The sun tickets are cheaper, because they are hotter and the sun is shining in your eyes during the fight. At a fight, you will first see the matador and his entourage parade into the ring. Then the bull is released and tested with a series of elaborate cape movements. Then, *picadores* mounted on horses chase after the bull and stab him with lances, which weaken him. The bleeding bull will charge the horses, but they wear padding to protect them from his horns. Next, the matador's assistants try to stick *banderillas* (sharp sticks) into the bull's shoulders. Finally, the matador approaches him on foot and begins the art of bullfighting. He uses a sword and a short red cape called a *muleta*, and encourages the bull to charge in a series of passes. The matador's movements are very close to the bull's horns and body, and can be quite exciting to watch. The fight concludes when the matador kills the bull with his sword, ideally with a single thrust. (In Portugal, the bulls are not killed in the ring, but in Spain they are).

Please note that Spanish people currently have mixed views about the 'sport' of bullfighting. In some parts of the country, the practice is outlawed because it is bloody and demonstrates animal cruelty. The bulls are bred for the ring, and prepared for their fight with cruel treatments that border on torture. However, supporters argue that it is an artistic element of Spanish culture and should be preserved as a cultural event. Whether or not you choose to attend a fight, or watch one on TV, you can appreciate the importance of the bulls in Spanish traditions.

JUNE 23: FEAST OF SAN JUAN

The night of June 23-24 is a unique celebration. This is the shortest night of the year, and is a festival that mixes light and darkness, fire and water. At beach towns throughout the region, people spend the whole evening on the sand eating and drinking around bonfires. Many people will attempt to jump three times over the fire, in what used to be a pagan superstition about purifying and burning away problems. At midnight, everyone jumps into the ocean, to wash away evil spirits. Some towns even have fireworks on this night. It is a fun and festive occasion not to be missed.

JULY 15: FIESTA DEL CARMEN

This is the feast of Our Lady of Mount Carmel, the patron saint of fishermen. So in ports throughout Spain and in coastal towns like Rota, Puerto, and Cádiz, there will be special activities and flotillas of boats in the harbor that carry an image of Mary.

EARLY AUGUST: HORSE RACES IN SANLÚCAR

Every August, in the nearby town of Sanlúcar de Barremeda, there is a series of horse races on the beach. The races, called *carreras de caballos de Sanlúcar*, have been held at this location since about 1845, so they are one of the oldest horse races in Spain. They are held on two different weekends and scheduled around the low tide on the Guadalquivir river, around 6:30 pm, and last until sunset, around 10 pm. The races are about 1 mile, so they only last a few moments, but there is a new race every 45 minutes. This is a great free event for the whole family. Enjoy a day at the beach, a beautiful sunset, and some thrilling horse races! More info in Part IV of this book.

AUGUST 15: ASSUMPTION (NATIONAL HOLIDAY)

This is the feast of the Assumption of Mary into heaven. Catholics believe that after her death, Mary's body and soul were taken into heaven. This is a religious feast celebrated throughout Spain and in other Catholic countries. Spanish churches will hold special Masses and events, and a majority of Spanish will attend Mass on this day. If it falls during the week, stores and businesses will be closed.

MID AUGUST

Every year, the town of Chipiona holds a wine festival in mid-August featuring their signature white wine, Moscatel. This festival is unique to Chipiona (about 20 minutes from base) and lasts about one week with tasting and wine education events, as well as promotions at local restaurants.

SEPTEMBER 8: VIRGIN OF MIRACLES

The feast of Virgen de los Milagros, the Virgin of Miracles, is a celebration in Puerto and a few other towns in Spain, but not in other local towns besides Puerto. The Virgin of Miracles is an alabaster statue with an interesting history.

MID SEPTEMBER

The town of Jerez de la Frontera celebrates their Festival de Otoño (Autumn Festival) every September when the grapes ripen for sherry production. This is a wonderful festival featuring everything that is unique to Jerez: sherry, flamenco, bulls, and horses. For a week there will be concerts, winery tours, sherry tastings, horse and flamenco shows. There will also be bullfights, but these can be found at various towns throughout the summer season.

OCTOBER 7: OUR LADY OF THE ROSARY

This is the Feast of Our Lady of the Rosary, which is the patron saint of the town of Rota and Cádiz. It is a feast in Rota, but will not be celebrated in other local towns. In Rota, the feast is celebrated with a week of activities, parades, and a ceremony that crowns a young woman "queen" of the celebration. Up to twenty other young women in festive dresses will be recognized as her court, and there will be a parade and a dancing celebration in the Plaza d'España. There has always been one lady representing the Spanish Navy, and another lady to represent the American military (usually a high school student). The whole community can be involved in this event.

OCTOBER 12: DÍA DE LA HISPANIDAD (NATIONAL HOLIDAY)

This is the feast of the Virgen de Pilar, Our Lady of the Pillar, patroness of Spain and the Hispanic world. It is a religious feast that is still celebrated nationally and called Día de la Hispanidad. There is a special military parade in Madrid. It also coincides with Columbus's discovery of the New World, so some people celebrate Columbus Day instead of the religious holiday. Either way, expect schools and businesses to be closed.

NOVEMBER 1: ALL SAINTS' DAY (NATIONAL HOLIDAY)

This is a religious feast celebrated throughout the Catholic world. On November 1, the feast of All Saints, most Spanish will attend church. On November 2, the Feast of All Souls, the Spanish will visit graveyards to leave flowers or gifts on the graves of their ancestors. Observation of the actual holiday with school and business closings is usually on one of these two dates.

DECEMBER 6: DÍA DE LA CONSTITUTIÓN (NATIONAL HOLIDAY)

This National Holiday recognizes the passage of the modern constitution on this date in 1978. After the death of dictator Francisco Franco, a new constitution was needed to recognize the newly-formed Parliament. This marks the beginning of Spain being a democracy and a constitutional monarchy. There are institutional events at all town halls and schools. Schools and businesses will be closed so people can enjoy time with their families. The holiday can sometimes be observed on the closest Monday or Friday.

DECEMBER 8: INMACULADA CONCEPCIÓN (NATIONAL HOLIDAY)

This is a religious feast celebrated throughout the Catholic world. It recognizes the Church teaching that Mary, the mother of Jesus, was conceived without sin. Most Spanish will attend church on this day, and there will be parades and processions around the main cathedrals. Because it falls so close to the celebration of Spain's Constitution Day, the two holidays are often celebrated as one long weekend, with people getting off work on both Friday and Monday. This long weekend is considered the beginning of the Christmas season in Spain. It's the weekend when Spanish families set up their nativity scenes, which are even more important to families than Christmas trees. Typically, you will not see decorations or Christmas activities until this date.

DECEMBER 25: CHRISTMAS/ NAVIDAD (NATIONAL HOLIDAY)

Like much of the world, the Spanish celebrate Christmas Day as a vacation from work, to enjoy time with family. The King delivers a message on TV around 9 pm on Christmas Eve. It is typical to attend church together on Christmas Eve, and then enjoy a long meal most of the night. Sometimes people return to have lunch with their families on Christmas Day, the 25th. However, gifts are not traditionally exchanged on this day. Adults may exchange gifts, but children's gifts are saved until January 6, and delivered not by Santa, but by the Three Kings.

There are several wonderful Christmas traditions that can be found throughout Spain for most of the month of December. The first is the Christmas Markets. Germany might be world-renowned for its hand-crafted items and crowded Christmas Markets, but Spain shares in this tradition too. Small towns like Rota will have a small market lasting only one weekend, which is like an outdoor fair. Vendors set up wooden stalls selling everything from fresh baked goods, jamón and cheese, hand-crafted jewelry, antiques, candy, and toys. There are usually a few rides, games, or activities for children. Larger cities like Sevilla will have several large markets in locations throughout the city, with much more food and handicraft options. Popular items include carved Nativity sets or religious figurines, and you can eat churros (fried sugary dough) with hot chocolate. Markets are closed during siesta, but reopen with well-lit stalls and rides that last into the night.

Another great Spanish Christmas tradition is the *Zambombas*. These are musical performances of Spanish Christmas carols, usually accompanied by flamenco dancers and the unique zambomba drum. Sometimes they take place in an auditorium, on a stage, with tickets sold in advance. Other more casual zambombas are in bars and open to anyone who walks by. Or they can be sung with friends together at home.

Finally, a unique tradition in Arcos de la Frontera and Medina Sidonia every December is the living nativity. For one day and night in December (usually the weekend before Christmas), the entire town will be transformed into a re-enactment of Bethlehem at the time of Christ's birth. Truckloads of dirt fill the town square to turn a parking lot into a dusty version of Palestine. Citizens of these towns set up stalls, fire pits, and action scenes with authentic costumes representing 1st century Jews, Roman soldiers, and all the main Biblical characters. Whether you go during the day or night, it is an impressive experience, but one that comes with lots of crowds and uphill walking.

STORES AND SHOPPING

Store hours can vary, depending on the time of year (slower during the winter months) or when the owner goes on vacation. Larger chain stores have longer and more predictable hours than a mom and pop stand. But in general, stores and businesses are open from about 10 am-1 pm, then they close for lunch and siesta. Stores re-open from about 5:30-8:30 pm. On Saturday, stores open in the morning, close for siesta, and often do NOT reopen in the evening. On Sundays, most stores are closed all day as the Spanish spend Sundays at church or with family.

In January and July, most stores throughout the whole country have special sales, *Rebajas*, with discounted prices. This can be a great time to shop for gifts or souvenirs like leather and pottery items, but you will find deals at clothing and novelty stores as well.

GROCERY STORES:

Shopping for food in Spain can be a little challenging, since all labels will be in Spanish. For the most part, larger grocery stores are similar to any chain store in the United States. You can always wander the aisles and eventually identify the product you need by the picture on the label. There are a few important differences to be aware of. First, carts and baskets usually appear to be locked up in the parking lot or at the store entrance. You need to insert a coin to use them. But don't worry, you are not being charged for the cart! You get your coin back when you return the cart to the line at the end of your trip. It's just a way of keeping the carts orderly so they won't be abandoned all over the parking lot. One thing you will be charged for is plastic bags. There are typically no baggers at the check-out lines. You bag your own groceries. Unless you bring your own bags, or put everything back into the cart, you will have to ask for bags: *bolsas*. Each one costs a few Euro cents, so you need to ask for a specific number of *bolsas* at the beginning of your order. The cashier will then scan them and give them to you so you can begin bagging.

Another big difference about European stores is that milk is not refrigerated and not kept near the other dairy products. Europeans use a different pasteurizing process, so their milk cartons can be stored at room temp until opened. Then they should be refrigerated after opening. Some grocery stores have fresh meat or seafood counters. You usually must take a number to be served. You will notice that the Spanish do not form lines. If there is no number system, they form a group around the counter, and as each new person walks up they ask, *"Quien es el ultimo?"* (Who is the last?) Someone will raise their hand, and then the newcomer knows they will be served after that person. If you don't ask the question or raise your hand, you could interfere with the system and take longer to get served. Grocery stores are great for getting a variety of assorted foods, but usually the best quality will be at smaller local stores specializing in each type of food.

- *Fruteria* is a local fruit and vegetable stand, and the best source of fresh produce at good prices. Rota is known for its tomatoes and squash. Chipiona is known for good oranges.

- *Panaderia* is a bakery, which mainly makes loaves of bread and sells snacks and convenience items. For richer desserts and pastries, go to a *pasteleria*.

- *Charcuteria* is a butcher, where various cuts of sausage, pork, jamón, chicken, etc. can be purchased. You may have to look up words for particular cuts or specialty requests before you go, or just use hand gestures. Litchfield's English Butcher in Chiclana imports a variety of British novelties and specialty cuts of meat. The owner currently delivers orders to the base once a month. Contact info: litch@hotmail.co.uk. You can also order cuts through the Commissary.

- *Pescadería* is the fish market. There is one in Rota, Puerto, and Cádiz, right near the docks where the fishing boats come in with the day's fresh catch. Seafood is sold by the kilo, and you may want to bring a dictionary to look up the names of different fish. Ask for it *limpio* if you want it cleaned and gutted.

- **Organic or Health Food** stores are not easy to find, but much of Spain's food is less processed and more natural than what is sold in the states. For truly organic food, go to Biolandia Tienda Ecologica (in Puerto), La Panacea (in Jerez) or La Alacena (in Cádiz). There are also some organic produce farms in the area, where you can place an order online, and either pick it up on location, or have it delivered to the base gate.

- **Carrefour, Hipercor, Lidl, and Alcampo** are chain grocery stores located in towns all around base with fresh produce, frozen and canned items, and beer and wine, as well as a limited selection of household goods, clothing, and cleaning products. They are sometimes compared to Wal-Mart, though much smaller.
- **Super Sol** is similar to Carrefour, though somewhat smaller—affordable food and some basic household goods, available in several locations near base. There are 2 in Rota.
- **Mercadona** is a chain grocery store with a large location in Puerto, and several smaller ones throughout the area—Rota and Costa Ballena. It has a fresh seafood counter, and all of the typical fresh and canned goods you would look for in a grocery store.
- **Makro**, in Puerto, is the only type of wholesale store in the area. It requires a membership, and is mostly intended for restaurant owners. You can save some money buying spices and dry goods in large quantities, but you must have adequate storage room in your kitchen for bulk items.
- **Costco** is now open in Sevilla. If you have a stateside membership, your card will still be honored here. If you do not yet have a membership, you will have to contact the store for details. You can use your EU drivers' license to get a new card.

BAZARS (CHINO STORES):

These are individual stores present in nearly every neighborhood with an inventory similar to the Dollar Tree or Dollar General. Although the sign typically says Bazar, locals call them Chino stores. The name is derived from the fact that the owners are typically Chinese, and many products are made in China. Visit them to get cheap items like toys, gifts, household goods, craft supplies, and even clothing. Each store is privately run and maintains its own unique inventory, so you never quite know what they will have, but the local chino store is a great place to search for a bargain, or for that one strange item you don't know where to find anywhere else.

GYPSY MARKETS:

They are called gypsy markets because they are usually run by the *gitanos*, or gypsy population. This is like an outdoor flea market, with each vendor setting up their own tent area and naming their own prices. Each local town hosts a Gypsy market one day every week, always on the same day and at the same location. Currently, the market can be found year-round, weather permitting:

- Jerez (Calle Hijuela de Las Coles), Mondays
- Chipiona (Avenida Félix Rodríguez de la Fuente), Mondays
- Puerto (end of Avenida de la Bajamar), Tuesdays
- Rota (Bus depot parking lot just outside and to the right of the Rota base gate), Wednesdays.

Gypsy markets are a great place to get new shoes, boots, purses, clothing, fabric, and curtains. You can also get fresh olives, spices, snails, nuts, and candy. You can attempt to haggle, but prices quoted to Americans are often higher than prices quoted to locals. The products are completely legal: vendors obtain a license and keep it displayed in their area. Police also patrol the grounds.

SHOPPING MALL LOCATIONS:

- **El Paseo Mall, Puerto**: Contains Toys R Us, Claire's, a large Carrefour, Zara Home, and multiple clothing and shoe stores. GPS coordinates: 36°36'58.5"N 6°12'42.2"W.
- **Luz Shopping Center, Jerez**: Contains Ikea, Bricor, Decathalon, Prenatal, and numerous clothing stores. There is also indoor laser tag and Go Karting here, and an outdoor pirate playground in the center area. It has several restaurants, including Muerde la Pasta, which is a great buffet with a huge indoor play area for kids. GPS coordinates: 36°41'40.1"N 6°09'35.1"W.
- **Bahia Sur in San Fernando:** contains El Corte Ingles. GPS coordinates: 36°27'42.9"N 6°12'07.8"W.
- **Las Dunas Mall in Sanlúcar**: Brand names like Guess, H&M, Tommy Hilfiger, and Mango. GPS coordinates: 36°45'09.5"N 6°20'18.6"W.

HOUSEHOLD GOODS:

- *Ferretería* is a local hardware store. They are usually very small shops, and each carries a slightly different inventory. But they generally have tools, hardware, outdoor equipment, and sometimes household items. There are several bigger ones in the Rota industrial area.

- **Ikea** in Jerez's Luz shopping center is just like any Ikea in the states: affordable furniture, rugs, curtains, and household décor that you must carry away and assemble yourself. There is a supervised play area where you may leave your children for 1 hour, and a cafeteria.

- **Bricor** in Jerez's Luz shopping center is like a combination of Bed Bath & Beyond and Michael's craft stores. They have a huge assortment of household appliances, tools and décor, as well as sections with hardware, paint, craft supplies, and some fabric.

- **Zara, or Zara Home** offers quality furnishings for bedroom, bathroom, living room, and table ware. Zara is the clothing line. Closest locations are El Paseo Mall in Puerto, or Area Sur (next to Luz Shopping Center) in Jerez.

- **El Corte Ingles** is a department store with sections including dishes, bedding, and home décor. Nearby locations are in Jerez, Cádiz, or the San Fernando Mall.

- **Furniture stores** are also in shorter supply in Spain than in the United States. Americans typically find Spanish furniture to be very expensive, though sometimes quite worth it for a hand-crafted item. The biggest furniture store in Rota is **Meubles Arjona**, in the industrial area, visible from the road towards Chipiona. You can also try **Muebles Marin** in Avenida San Fernando (in Rota). Furniture is also sold at **Ikea** or **Jysk**, in Jerez's Luz Shopping center.

CLOTHING STORES:

- There are numerous small shops throughout Rota and Puerto specializing in particular brands, styles, seasons, or formal clothing. The Spanish generally dress very smartly, with class, even to run every day errands. Ask a local for a good recommendation for *moda* (clothing).
- **Al Campo, Carrefour, or Gypsy Markets** are good places to find cheap simple clothing and accessories for children or adults.
- **El Corte Ingles** is a department store like Sears or Macy's, with locations throughout Spain. The closest are in Jerez, Cádiz, and the San Fernando Bahia Sur Mall.
- **Primark** is a British brand of affordable children's, women's, and men's clothing. Closest location is Jerez's Area Sur (right next to Luz shopping center).
- **The El Paseo Mall** in Puerto has clothing stores like a large Carrefour, C&A (like Old Navy), PePe Jeans, and Mayoral (children's clothes). There is also a Claire's store for jewelry and accessories (and ear piercings).
- **Luz Shopping Center** in Jerez has several clothing stores, as well as outlet stores for brands like Mango and El Corte Ingles.
- **Las Dunas Mall** in Sanlúcar has Guess, H&M, Tommy Hilfiger, and Mango, among others.

SPORTS:

- **Decathlon** is a huge sports store with locations in Puerto and Jerez's Luz Shopping Center. They have every kind of sports and outdoor equipment and apparel, for adults or children. They also do repairs for bikes, tennis rackets, etc.
- **Nike Factory Store** in Jerez's Luz shopping center is the place to get a properly fitted shoe.
- **Intersports** in El Paseo Mall, Puerto, is a good source of athletic apparel, *moda deportiva*.

BABY ITEMS:

- **Gypsy Markets** are a great place to get adorable baby clothing and shoes. Spanish styles are a little different from American styles, so they are sometimes pricey, but very charming.
- **Prenatal** is a chain store specializing in maternity and baby products. The closest is in Jerez's Luz Shopping Center.
- **Toys R Us** is located in the El Paseo Mall in Puerto
- **Toy Planet** is a small store in Jerez's Luz shopping center with a variety of cheap toys and accessories.

BEAUTY SALONS:

- The **Beauty Salon** at the NEX offers haircuts, styling, and coloring services, as well as manicures, pedicures, and waxing.
- Azul Salon, just outside the Fuentabravia gate, is popular for manicures and nail design. They also offer pedicures, hair coloring and styling services, massages, and facials. Some English is spoken, and monthly specials are offered. They also have a location in Rota.
- The **Sanlúcar Fish Spa** is a unique experience of receiving a pedicure from a pool of tiny fish that nibble all the rough skin from your feet. They also offer a full range of spa and massage services, facials, hair, nail, and skin treatments, including chocolate therapy. Address is Calle Hermano Fermín, Local N°6 in Sanlúcar.
- There is a full-service spa in Rota's **Hotel Espadaña**, and several spas in Costa Ballena.
- There are always Americans on base with home businesses offering hair styling services, nail designs, and make-up, as well as massages. But these depend on who is stationed here, and change frequently.

CRAFTING SUPPLIES:

- Craft stores like Michael's and JoAnn's do not seem to exist in this area, so it is always difficult to find specific fabric, thread, yarn, and crafting items. The chino stores all carry an assortment of basic craft items. Sometimes specialty items can be ordered online. Michael's does not ship to APO addresses, but the following stores do: AC Moore, Hobby Lobby, Jo-Ann, Oriental Trading, and Party City.
- Fabric, tablecloths, curtains, and ribbons can be found at **gypsy markets** (ordered by the meter), or **Ikea** in Jerez.
- **Bricor** has a small selection of paints, craft supplies, and accessories like googly eyes, pipe cleaners, popsicle sticks, etc.
- **EN Home Markets** in Puerto (near Casa) and Jerez (near Leroy Merlin) has a variety of craft supplies, including yarn.
- **MerkAsia** in Jerez's Luz Shopping Center sells costumes, accessories, and beads, as well as crochet and yarn supplies.
- Baking and fondant supplies are found at **Megasilvita** in Rota.

ELECTRONICS: (remember everything sold here will be 220 volts, unless you go shopping in Gibraltar)

- **Worten**, in Jerez's Luz Shopping center, is a large electronics store similar to Best Buy or Circuit City.
- **El Corte Ingles** is a department store whose electronics section includes everything from TV's, computers, phones, kitchen appliances, and cameras.
- You can also find items in smaller stores in Rota's industrial area.

GARDENING SUPPLIES:

Viveros is the Spanish word for a greenhouse or garden center. There are many in the area, but the most accessible is **Viveros El Lago,** just outside the Puerto gate, off the first roundabout. It does not offer the best prices, but has an excellent selection of seeds, indoor and outdoor flowers, decorative pottery, fencing, soil, fertilizer, and some silk flowers too. They also sell live Christmas trees in December. There is a much larger Viveros in Chipiona (heading toward Sanlúcar) called **Rivera Garden,** which is like a warehouse full of garden furniture, patio accessories, and a wide variety of plants and seeds, as well as a cafeteria and children's playground.

FERIA DRESSES:

New feria dresses can cost 200 Euros and up. They are custom made and tailored to fit. New dresses can be found at several shops in Rota or Puerto, and of course there is a good selection in Sevilla. For more affordable options:

- Second-hand dresses can be purchased at the store in Rota, **Cambalache de Rota.**
- **Gypsy markets** sell Feria dresses, shoes, and accessories for adults and children starting in March.
- The Rota community uses the Yard Sale Facebook page to sell and exchange dresses every spring.
- The NEX now processes orders for Feria dresses throughout the spring.

CERAMICS:

Spanish pottery is gorgeous, and one of the most popular gift and souvenir items. It can be shipped to the States, but make sure it is carefully bubble wrapped, packed in newspaper, and possibly even shipped in double boxes. The pottery is all hand-painted, but chips easily and is very fragile. There is a selection at the NEX, which is gathered from all over Spain, and the selection changes constantly. However, their prices are not very competitive. For more affordable and authentic selection, visit the following locations:

- **Viveros El Lago**, just outside the Puerto gate, has a great selection of all kinds of pottery, from serving platters to specialty dishes to flower pots and planters.
- **Triana** is the ceramics district of Sevilla, about 1.5 hours from base. Prices and selection are good here. There are numerous shops along the streets San Jacinto and Calle San Jorge. Parking is available in Plaza del Altazano. See samples from one shop at www.ceramicatriana.com.
- **La Rambla** is THE location for pottery shopping, but it is near Cordoba, about 2.5 hours from base. The town is renowned for hand-crafted items, bright painted patterns, and the largest selection with the best prices. You can take tours to learn about the pottery-making process, or just spend the day shopping. Many stores close for siesta from 2-5 pm. Samples from one shop can be viewed at www.ceramicaeltiti.com.
- Ceramics from El Titi in La Rambla are also available in Arcos, about 40 minutes from base. They are more expensive than in La Rambla, but the location is more convenient. It is called **Arx-Arcis**, located at Calle Marques de Torresoto #11.

DINING OUT IN SPAIN

First, remember that restaurant hours are dramatically different than in the United States. 10 am is breakfast time, so it is easy to get toast or bocadillos or tortillas in the morning. However, most places don't open for lunch until 1 pm. Then they close around 4, and do not open for dinner until about 8 pm. If you see people enjoying afternoon coffee or drinks at a restaurant, it does not mean they are serving hot food. Usually, only drinks and cold tapas are available until 8 pm. It takes time to get used to this dining schedule, so try to plan accordingly, or call first to see when the kitchen opens.

Next, you may be confused by the amount of bars, and the quantity of people sitting in them all day. A place named 'Bar' or 'Bar Restaurant' is really more like a café. Sure, you can get a beer or wine there, but most clients will be drinking coffee or eating small simple meals like plates of jamón and cheese. For this reason, they open in the morning, and remain open most of the day.

An establishment called a *Venta* is translated to roadhouse, and is more like a diner. These family-run restaurants offer a small number of house specialties—usually simple, but very tasty dishes like tortillas, garlic chicken, or fried seafood. They are usually open for lunch and dinner, but under Spanish hours only.

Spanish meals are slow and leisurely. Waiters expect to leave you quiet and undisturbed at your table, so they typically will not come by to take your order or deliver the check unless you make eye contact or call them over. They also will not bring the check until you ask for it: *'la cuenta, por favor.'* Water is not free, unless you order tap water: *agua del grifo*. Carbonated water is *con gas*, regular flat bottled water is *sin gas*. Refills are not free, and soda is sometimes more expensive than beer or wine. A basket of bread and crackers (*picos*) or a plate of olives is typically placed on the table. They are complimentary, but you sometimes see a charge of 2-3 Euros on the bill for *pan y picos*. Butter is not usually served with bread. Instead, sprinkle it with olive oil and a little salt. Sauces like ketchup or hot sauce are not usually on the table, so you have to ask for ketchup (a purely American topping), mayonnaise, or *salsa picante* (hot sauce). Or consider bringing packets of your own favorites, like ranch dressing. Portions in Spain are usually rich and filling, but smaller than what is served in American restaurants, so there typically are not leftovers. However, if you wish to have something wrapped up to take home, simply ask for it *para llevar.*

Many menus list different portion sizes, which you must indicate when you order. *Tapas* are very small portions, usually just a few bites, meant as an appetizer, or a snack to enjoy with your beer. The next size, ½ *ration*, is a lunch portion or a light dinner. This might be a few ounces of meat or seafood, a nice quantity for one person. The largest size, *ration*, is a full-sized meal, sometimes with enough to share between two people.

Payment at many restaurants, especially small bars or ventas, should typically be in Euro cash. Credit cards are usually accepted at larger restaurants, touristy areas, or for large purchases. Technically, credit cards are accepted at most establishments, but it is amazing how many places of business do not have a credit card machine, or how often the machine goes offline and can't be used because of technical problems. If you discover upon receiving the bill that you don't have enough cash, you will be directed to the nearest ATM (*el cajero automático*). You can usually use American debit cards in any Spanish ATM. Your company will probably charge you a service fee for the transaction. When you withdraw cash, always request it "without conversion" or you will be given a worse exchange rate.

A Spanish value added tax (VAT) of about 20% is automatically imposed on all restaurant bills. For that reason, and because waiters are paid their own wages, tipping is not very high at restaurants throughout Spain. The locals never tip for just a drink, and only leave pocket change at a typical restaurant. Restaurant owners are responsible for covering waiters' wages and health benefits, so they do not survive on tips. For average service at an average restaurant, it is common to round up the bill or leave 2-5 Euros on the table. (For example, leaving 40 Euros when the total bill was 37 Euros). For better service, better food, or an expensive restaurant, of course you may leave more. For bad service, it is common not to leave anything. But the Spanish are aware that Americans are more used to tipping, so it is only 'expected' in touristy areas.

For more information about the kinds of food typical to menus in this region, see Part III of this book.

LEARNING SPANISH

Whether you choose to brush up on Spanish before you move here, or wait until after you arrive, it is recommended that all Americans stationed on base learn at least the minimal phrases necessary to get through everyday life: ordering at a restaurant, asking for directions, requesting help in a store, etc. If you remain on base, you can conduct most of your business in English and get by knowing very little Spanish. But whenever you go in town, you will get much more out of the culture, and have a better overall experience, if you learn some basic Spanish. Most Spanish people in the area speak very little English, so it will be easier for you to make local friends if you can hold a bilingual conversation.

> **The Fleet and Family Support Center on base offers beginner Spanish classes for free! The classes meet twice a week for a few months at a time, and are a good place to start if you don't know any Spanish, or never took a language class before. To sign up, contact the base Fleet and Family Support Center.**

A quick note on Spanish as it is spoken in Spain: it is different from Mexican or South American Spanish. Most of the grammar and sentence structure is the same, but there are tons of words that are completely different, and a Spanish person will not recognize Mexican vocabulary. There is also a different accent. Here in Southern Spain, there is a strong accent, similar to a Texan drawl. If you learned to speak Spanish elsewhere, you will probably be understood, but you may need to speak slowly or repeat yourself. Conversely, if you learn from a local speaker here, you may not always be understood in Madrid or other Spanish-speaking parts of the world. In this area, J is pronounced as an H sound, and Z is pronounced as TH. So the town of Jerez is pronounced 'Hair-eth.'

There are many ways to learn a language, and some of them are very affordable. Some people teach themselves with phrase books, flashcards, or apps that present new pictures and vocabulary every day. Duolingo is a great, free app that is useful for learning vocabulary. Some people get by using Google Translate to enter phrases from either language and get a translation so you can write down a note or a phrase to show someone. A very effective (but somewhat expensive) tool is the Rosetta Stone program. This is useful if you have a background in high school Spanish or a similar language, because it will teach you lots of vocabulary and verbs, but will not explain the grammar rules or verb conjugations. There are similar off-brand programs that use the same teaching style as Rosetta Stone for a lower price. I completed Rosetta Stone Level 1 before moving here, and even though I still consider myself a beginner, my 'Spanglish' is usually enough to get by, and I get very positive responses from the Spanish, simply for making the effort to speak. They are usually very eager to teach you, and offer corrections kindly.

Another option is to join a conversation group or hire a tutor once you arrive. There are plenty of English-speaking Spanish teachers in the area around base, and they offer group or individual classes to help you pick up the language at your own pace. Prices vary depending on group size, but expect prices of at least 10 Euros per hour, and a meeting at least once a week. In the end, constant practice is what will make you more fluent, so if you truly want to learn, surround yourself with the Spanish environment, watch Spanish TV, and challenge yourself to speak in Spanish, even when the other person understands some English.

USEFUL SPANISH PHRASES

Yes .... Sí
No .... No
OK ....Vale
Good morning/day .... Buenos días
Excuse me.. Perdone
I'm sorry .... Lo siento
Please .... Por Favor
Thank you ....Gracias
You're welcome .... De nada
See you later .... Hasta luego
Give me .... Déme
I would like .... Quisiera
I want .... Quiero…
I need ....Necesito…
I like .... Me gusta…
Name ....Nombre
My name is … (I call myself…) .... Me llamo …
Do you have …? ....¿Tiene usted… ?
Where is…? .... ¿Donde esta…?
When? ....¿Cuando?
What time is it? .... ¿Qué hora es?
What? .... ¿Que?
What did you say? .... ¿Cómo?
How much is it? .... ¿Cuánto cuesta?
Bathroom .... Servicio, Aseo, or Baño
Exit .... La Salida
To the right .... A la derecha
To the left .... A la izquierda
Straight ahead ....Todo recto
Now..Ahora
Later...Más tarde
Today ....Hoy
Tomorrow .... Mañana
Yesterday .... Ayer
Morning .... La mañana
Afternoon ....La tarde
Night .... La noche

Inside ....Dentro
Outside ....Fuera
Open ....Abierto
Closed ....Cerrado
Good ....Bueno
Bad ....Malo
More ....Más
Less ....Menos
Too much ....Demasiado
Big ....Grande
Small ....Pequeño
Cold ....Frío
Hot.. Calor (weather), Caliente (food)
Do you speak English? .... ¿Habla usted ingles?
I speak a little Spanish .... Hablo un poco de español
Menu .... La carta
Check/ Bill ....La cuenta
Credit card .... La tarjeta de crédito
Cash ....Efectivo
Beer .... La cervesza
Wine ....El vino
Juice .... El zumo
Coffee with frothed milk .... Café con leche
Black coffee ....Café solo
Breakfast .... El desayuno
Lunch.. La comida
Dinner ....La cena
Parking lot ....El Aparcamiento
Town Hall ....El Ayuntamiento
My name is .... Me llamo...
Pleased to meet you ....Encantado de conocerle
I don't understand ....No entiendo
Help ....Ayuda
I am lost ....Me he perdido

METRIC CONVERSIONS

Like most of the world, Spain uses the metric system for weights and measures. America is one of the only countries that uses the so-called 'Standard' system. So you cannot expect any Spanish person to understand pounds, feet, or miles. Instead, you will have to get used to using (or at least guessing) at metric quantities when you want something.

1 kilo = 2.2 pounds
1 meter = 1.1 yards, or 3.3 feet
1 kilometer = 0.62 miles
1 mile = 1.6 kilometers
60 kilometers/hour (speed limit on most of base) = 37.3 miles/hour
120 kilometers/hour (speed limit on highways) = 74 miles/hour
1 liter = 1.06 quarts (gas prices are listed in Euros/liter)
1 gallon = 3.785 liters
1 cup liquid = 240 ml
330 mL (soda/beer can size)= 11.2 oz
750 mL (wine bottle size) = 25.4 oz
1 cup dry (flour or rice) = 150 grams
1 oz = 30 g (to convert to grams, multiply ounces by 30)
1 foot = 30 cm (to convert to centimeters, multiply inches by 2.5)

TEMPERATURE CONVERSIONS

	Temperature Fahrenheit	Temperature Celsius
Water Freezes:	32° F	0° C
Cold day:	40° F	4° C
Room Temp:	68° F	20° C
Hot Day:	90° F	32° C
Water boils:	212° F	100° C
Bake:	350° F	180° C
	400° F	200° C
Broil:	500° F	260° C

PART III: FOOD

Introduction to Spanish Food
Common Menu Items
Spanish Dishes, and Recipes
Restaurants in Rota
   Bar Gomez (Spanish Breakfast Sandwiches)
   Badulaque (Spanish Food, Beach Views)
   100 Montaditos (Sandwiches, Beach Views)
   Parilla Los Argentinos (Grilled Meats)
   Las Tinajas (Spanish Grilled Specialties)
   Bar La Feria (Spanish Food, Flamenco Shows)
   Takiko's (Japanese/Chinese, Base Delivery)
   La Dolce Vita (Italian, Harbor Views)
   Pizza Y Pasta (Delivery To Base)
   Shanza (Indian Dishes, Delivery to Base)
   La Almadraba (Spanish Grilled and Seafood Specialties)
Restaurants in Puerto
   Venta El Nene (Tortillas and American Breakfast)
   Parilla Bailey's (Grilled Specialites, Children's Playground)
   El Ultimo (Bar Food, Fuentabravia)
   Venta La Rufana (Family Owned Roadhouse)
   Crêfondue (Fondue and Crepes, Ocean Views)
   Blanco Paloma (Pizza and Pasta with Ocean Views)
   Bar Jamon (Upscale Spanish Cuisine)
   Venta La Feria (Huge Paella Varieties)
   Little Italy (Pizza, Pasta, And Children's Play Area)
   Bamboo Sushi (Great Sushi And Sashimi)
   Shamrock (Traditional Irish Pub Food)
   El Sitio De Vélez (Upscale Spanish Cuisine)

INTRODUCTION TO SPANISH FOOD

First of all, if you expect Spanish food to be anything like Mexican food or Tex-Mex, you will be surprised to discover that tacos and taquitos are foreign here, and considered more American than anything else. Spanish cuisine centers on the Mediterranean diet—lots of fresh produce, seafood, olive oil, and pork. Spanish food is typically seasoned only with onions, peppers, tomatoes, garlic, and oil, but all those products have a much stronger flavor here than in the States. Sherry wine is also frequently used in food preparation. So instead of being bland, the food typically has a deep, rich flavor. The Spanish do not usually like spicy dishes.

You may be pleasantly surprised by the freshness and quality of Spanish ingredients. In America, we are used to a great deal of processed food. In Spain, it is still traditional to shop at the local produce stand, bakery, meat market, and fish market, so food comes to you much fresher and with much less packaging or preservatives. The produce has much more flavor, and local produce will make even simple dishes taste great. Fresh loaves of bread can be purchased at the *panaderia*, but they will only last for a day before becoming stale. Fresh fish can be purchased whole from the market, the same day it comes off the fishing boats. However, if you are specifically looking for organic, hormone-free, or free-range food you may need to do some research. There are a few farms in the area that provide organic vegetables or meat, but this is not a widespread demand in Spanish culture, so you may need to go directly to the farm. A limited selection of organic vegetables and meats are available on base at the commissary.

In this region, seafood is more plentiful than anything else, so restaurants usually serve a variety of fish dishes. Fish is often served whole, with head, tail, and bones. Seafood can also be fried, either whole (in the case of small items like sardines) or in pieces, like calamari. The frying process here is different from the American south. The batter is much lighter and thinner, closer to tempura. Inland, you will find more meat dishes, including rabbit and venison.

Finally, if you are vegetarian, vegetable dishes and salads are easy to find, but vegetarian main dishes are less common. You can ask for a dish *vegetarian*, but you may still have bacon pieces sprinkled on a 'vegetarian' dish.

COMMON MENU ITEMS

A la plancha: Grilled

A la roteña: 'Rota style,' meaning baked fish prepared in a stew of
     tomatoes, onions, peppers, garlic, black pepper, and wine

Aceite: Oil, usually Olive Oil

Aceitunas: Olives

Adobado: Marinated

Agua: Water

Ajo: Garlic

Almejas: Clams

Arranque: traditional Rota specialty, a sauce made of tomatoes, stale
     bread, garlic, oil, peppers, and salt, usually served with bread

Arroz: Rice

Atún: Tuna

Bacalao: Cod

Bebidas: Beverages

Bocadillo: Sandwich made with a large crusty bread bun, topped with
     meat, cheese, and/or tomatoes

Boquerones: Sardines

Café Con Leche: Coffee with frothed milk

Carne: Meat

Cebolla: Onion

Cerdo: Pork

Cerveza: Beer (the most common is Cruzcampo, a cheap beer tasting
     similar to Pabst Blue Ribbon)

Champiñón: Mushroom

Chocos or Sepia: Cuttlefish, a kind of squid

Chorizo: Spiced Sausage, can be fresh or dried

Con: With (as in: *con queso*, with cheese)

Croquetas: Fried Miniballs, filled with cheese, fish, ham, or veggies

Crudo: Raw

El Postre: Dessert

Ensalada: Salad

Espaguetis: Spaghetti

Fideos: Noodles

Filete: Steak (beef or pork)

Frito/ Fritas: Fried

Fruta: Fruit

Gambas: Prawns, or very large shrimp

Gazpacho: Fresh Tomato Soup, made with garlic, peppers, vinegar, olive oil, and bread—all pureed and served cold. Sometimes topped with cucumbers, egg, or jamón.

Hamburguesa: Hamburger

Helado: Ice Cream

Hielo: Ice

Huevo: Egg

Jamón: Cured Ham, very thinly sliced. *Jamón serrano* is cheaper and fattier. *Jamón iberico* is more expensive, lean and flavorful.

La Sopa: Soup

Lomo: Loin

Lubina: Sea Bass—a rich, white fish

Montadito: Small Sandwich, a roll or toast topped with meat, cheese, and/or tomatoes

Paella: fancy dish of rice mixed with a variety of seafood, meat, vegetables, and saffron seasonings

Pan: Bread

Papas: Potatoes (usually sliced or cubed and fried)

Perrito: Hot Dog

Pez Espada: Swordfish

Pimientos: Peppers

Pollo: Chicken

Pulpo: Octopus

Queso: Cheese (There are numerous varieties, but Manchego—cured sheep cheese—is the most common.)

Salado: Salted

Salmonete: Red Mullet Fish (not salmon)

Salsa: Sauce or Gravy (not typically spicy)

Sin: Without (as in *sin carne*, without meat)

Solomillo: Tenderloin

Té: Tea

Ternera: Beef (or Veal)

Tortilla: Omelet of potatoes, eggs, and olive oil fried and then slowly cooked to make a soft and delicious dish that looks like a pie, and can be served whole or by the slice.

Urta: Rockfish (Rota's local specialty)

Vino: Wine (Red is Tinto, White is Blanco)

Zumo: Juice

SPANISH DISHES, AND HOW TO PREPARE THEM

<u>TAPAS</u>: The word *tapas* means 'lid.' One theory to the origin of the word claims that a bar owner placed pieces of toast on his wealthy patron's glass, so the flies would not get into the drink. Soon he started topping his toast with seafood, meat, or cheese. Tapas are basically Spanish appetizers, or a small plate with just a few bites of flavorful food. Tapas are designed as a tasty accompaniment to an afternoon or evening cocktail, but you can also make them into a meal if you go 'tapas hopping' with friends. This means visiting several restaurants in one night, ordering a few plates of tapas at each one, and then continuing along until everyone is full. It's a good way to taste some of the signature dishes from several different restaurants, without spending much money. Usually, friends who go tapas hopping pool their money at the beginning of the night, and use the cash to pay at each restaurant, so everyone can share the dishes and there is no need to split checks. Cold tapas are available in the late afternoon or early evening, and might include potato salad, some tasty meat and cheese, small squares of tortilla, or chilled seafood. These are wonderful in the summer, especially accompanied with a cool drink. Hot tapas are usually only available at lunch or dinner hours, and might include meatballs, fried seafood, or a small hamburger. A traditional tapas bar has standing room only, and often serves the tapas on napkins with toothpicks. If you sit down at a table and order tapas from there, you will pay a higher price. Each dish will make you want to have just one more drink, and with that drink you'll want to order another dish... so go ahead and point to some unknown items on the menu, and see what delicious bites they bring you. Tapas are different in every region of Spain, and at every restaurant. If you want to make your own, buy a tapas cookbook (in English) and experiment to discover some of your favorites. One of my favorites is on the next page.

PORK, PEPPER, AND MELTED CHEESE TOASTS (MONTADITOS)

Red Pepper
Olive Oil, Salt, Pepper
Fresh Bread
Jamón
Soft cheese (like Brie or Camembert).

First, thinly slice half a red pepper, and sauté in oil, with salt and pepper, just a few minutes until it is soft. Next, slice several pieces of fresh bread. Top each with a thin slice of jamón (cured ham), two slices of the cooked pepper, and a small wedge of soft cheese. Place under a hot broiler for about 1 minute, until the cheese melts and the bread becomes crispy. Serve hot. The blend of textures and flavors is delightful.

CROQUETAS: These are common items on any bar or restaurant menu. It may be translated as 'chicken nugget,' but a croquette is actually a doughy mixture that can contain chicken, tuna, spinach, or cheese. It is formed into bite-sized balls, then dipped in egg and breadcrumbs, and fried in oil. They will be softer than meatballs or chicken nuggets, but are still usually popular with children, and an easy affordable item to order if there is no kids' menu.

EMPANADAS: Unlike in Mexico, *empanadas* from Northern Spain are dough squares filled with meat, peppers, and cooked eggs. The top is then brushed with egg yolk and baked in the oven, so it is served like a pie.

EMPANADILLAS: a circle of dough filled with cooked meat and veggies, then folded in half and fried in oil. In this region, it is also common for them to be stuffed with tuna. They are eaten as a tapa, or appetizer.

TORTILLA: This is NOT Mexican tortilla bread, but delicious, moist Spanish tortilla! Tortilla is one of the most common dishes in Spain, and every family has their own style and unique recipe. It can be made simply with potatoes, onions, and eggs fried in olive oil, (which is the traditional tortilla de patatas), or you can add meat, peppers, and/or vegetables for more flavor. It is usually served as a wedge, resembling a piece of pie, or in small squares as tapas. You can also eat tortilla on a sandwich roll. Even if your first attempt at cooking it is not successful, keep trying! Once you find the right temperature and consistency, and master flipping it out of the pan, it is an easy and delicious dish to prepare.

TORTILLA DE PATATAS RECIPE:

1 Pound of Potatoes
1 Onion
4 Eggs, beaten

Slice the potatoes and onions very thinly. Start by frying them at high heat, then reduce the heat to cook them slowly. After adding the beaten eggs to the skillet, wait a few minutes for the eggs to set. Then, carefully using a large plate held firmly over the frying pan, you flip the entire tortilla on the plate, and then slide it gently back into the frying pan to cook a few minutes more on the other side. Serve warm or cold.

OLIVES AND OLIVE OIL: Spain is the world's largest olive producer, and the hills and mountains not far from base are covered in olive trees. The production of olive oil goes back to Roman times, when it was recognized for health and preservative properties. Now, it is primarily used for cooking. Olive oil should be dark and thick for maximum flavor and aroma. It breaks down from exposure to air and sunlight, so it should be stored in a dark, cool place in a solid (not glass) container. It is drizzled on almost every dish, hot or cold, and used in place of all other oils in cooking. (Never mix it with another oil). Olives are usually picked while still green, when they are firm, and then washed and brined in vinegar infused with garlic, herbs, or other flavors. They are usually served with the pit (*el hueso*) inside.

GAZPACHO: Gazpacho is a very common Spanish soup. It is made with fresh tomatoes, garlic, and often cucumbers, and always served cold. It can be served with a variety of toppings, such as croutons, chopped cucumbers, jamón, or chopped hard boiled eggs. The flavor is similar to a pico de gallo salsa—very fresh, and extremely refreshing, especially on a hot day in Spain. Another version found closer to Cordoba is *salmorejo*. This uses similar ingredients, but is much thicker because it uses more dried bread. *Salmorejo* is consumed either as a soup or a sauce for other dishes. A local dish using similar ingredients is *arranque*. This is a Rota specialty, a thick tomato sauce served with bread at many local restaurants. Arranque is made from fresh tomatoes, peeled and seeded, mixed with stale bread, garlic, oil, green peppers, and salt. It is served fresh and cold, and is a very healthy and refreshing dish!

GAZPACHO RECIPE:

3 Pounds Fresh Tomatoes, Peeled and Seeded
1 Seeded Green Pepper
2 Garlic Cloves
2 Pieces of Toast
4 Tbls. Olive Oil
4 Tbls. Sherry Vinegar
2/3 Cup Tomato Juice
1 ¼ Cups Cold Water

Toss all ingredients into the blender. Because it's a cold soup, you don't have to cook it! You just put it in the fridge for a few hours or overnight and let the flavors mix. Best served within 1 day.

PIMENTÓN: is a very common Spanish spice which is often translated as Paprika. Pimentón Dulce is actually Smoked Paprika, and Pimentón Picante is like Chili Powder. It can be used in a wide variety of dishes, from roasted meat to soups and stews. Pimentón dulce is not spicy, but almost sweet and smoky, giving food a very earthy flavor. Pimentón picante is usually used sparingly.

CARACOLES (SNAILS): You may be surprised to learn that snails are commonly eaten in Spain, especially in the spring or summer. You can order *caracoles*—cups of the tiny snails still in their shells—from bars and restaurants. They are boiled, salted, and served in a tomato sauce. You will see numerous Spanish sitting at tables with a tiny fork or toothpick, twisting the cooked snails out of their shells. You can buy snails for yourself from Gypsy markets or farmer's markets. It is not recommended that you gather the snails yourself, although you will see plenty of Spanish children doing this, particularly on the rocks near the beach. Those are called *burgaos*. If you gather wild snails, they need to be purged in a clean controlled environment for about a week before they are cooked. The larger snails—*cabrillas*—are also popular. Finally, *cañaillas* have a small conch shell, and can be purchased by the kilo from fish markets. They are cleaned, boiled in salted water, and served in a similar way, but have a much tougher chewier texture.

GAMBAS: Shrimp are common in Andalusian dishes, as they are plentiful off the Atlantic coast. They can be boiled and served cold on a salad or as a tapas, or they are sometimes baked in a tray of garlic butter that is served hot in an earthenware dish, with plenty of bread to soak up the sauce. *Gambas*, or their even larger relative, the *langostino* (prawn) usually come with shell, legs, eyes, tentacles, and all! It may take a while to get used to your food staring at you, but you can just remove the heads and shells before eating.

GAMBAS AL AJILLO (GARLIC PRAWNS):

Remove heads and legs of 16 large raw Prawns.
Heat 4 Tbls. Olive Oil in a frying pan.
Add 3 finely chopped Garlic Cloves,
and a pinch of Red Pepper Flakes (optional).
After 1 minute, add raw prawns, with tails, and fry for 3-4 minutes.
Garnish with fresh Parsley.
Serve with crusty Bread to soak up the sauce.

PAELLA: Paella is a Spanish celebration dish, served to large groups in backyard gatherings or parties. It is a mixture of rice, broth, seafood, meat, or vegetables, all slowly cooked in an enormous flat paella pan, traditionally over an open charcoal flame. Saffron is the dish's essential spice, which turns the rice yellow and gives it a distinct flavor. It is harvested by hand from purple crocus flowers, with only 1 tiny thread per bloom, so it is a costly spice sold in small vials. Use a large pinch of several threads to make each dish. In Andalusia, paella has seafood and snails. In other areas of the country they prefer meat paella with Chorizo sausage, chicken, and/or pork. Spanish rice is a short grain called Bola, but it is not widely available in the States, so you can use arborio or sushi rice if you are making your own. Do not stir, as this will make the rice sticky. You can use a wide paella dish over a stove burner, as long as you slowly rotate the pan after adding the rice to achieve even cooking.

TO MAKE YOUR OWN PAELLA:

Choose About 2-3 Pounds of Assorted Meat or Seafood
1 Cup of Green Beans or Peas
3 Tomatoes (Peeled and Seeded)
2 Onions
1 Red Pepper
2-3 Cloves Garlic
3 ¾ Cups Chicken Broth
Saffron and Pimentón Dulce seasonings
1 ¾ Cups Paella Rice (Bola)
Optional Garnishes: Chopped Green Olives, Fresh Parsley,
Or Lemon Wedges

Cook any fish, shrimp, mussels or other seafood separately. Chop up vegetables and meat, then fry them in a paella pan with several Tbls. Olive oil and a sprinkle of pimentón dulce. Add chicken broth, a generous pinch of saffron, and season with salt, pepper, and smoked paprika (pimentón dulce). Once boiling, stir in paella rice. Cook over medium-high heat for about 20 minutes *without stirring*, rotating the pan every few minutes, until liquid is absorbed. Add fish in when adding the rice; arrange other cooked seafood on top after cooking. Sprinkle with chopped green olives, or fresh parsley, and serve with lemon wedges. Enjoy your paella!

JAMÓN: The Spanish use every part of the pig, so it is common to see large haunches of pig legs—with the foot still attached—hanging in bars and grocery stores. These have been salted and cured for at least a year. *Jamón serrano* is the most common. It is thinly sliced and served on everything from tapas to sandwiches to salads, similar to Italian prosciutto. It comes from white pigs, and is very fatty. *Jamón ibérico* is made from the special breed of black-hoofed pigs, who are raised on a free-range diet of acorns to improve the meat's texture and flavor. The black hoof is often left on the haunch to demonstrate the higher quality. This meat has a deeper red color, much lower fat content, and has a great texture from being cured longer. The *ibérico* is more expensive, and not served on a basic sandwich or salad.

SAUSAGE: Pork is a huge staple in Spanish cooking, so it is no surprise that there are a variety of pork sausages used in different dishes. The most common is red *chorizo*, named for the flavorful and somewhat spicy *choricero* chili pepper that gives it the unique color and flavor. Chorizo can be purchased raw from a butcher shop and used in many stews and cooked dishes. Cured chorizo is sold in long batons. It is then thinly sliced and served as tapas, with cheese and/or bread. *Dulce* is sweeter, while *picante* is hot and spicy. If you order an Iberian or mixed meat platter from a restaurant, you will sample both kinds of chorizo, some jamón, and possibly another kind of sausage—*morcón*—similar to salami. One less common sausage, typically only found in soups or stews, is *morcilla*, which is blood sausage. It is black from boiled pig's blood, and has a very strong flavor and texture. Finally, white sausages such as *salchichón* are dry and chewy, typically sold covered with a white powdery substance, which is residual bacteria and safe to eat.

ENSALADA DE PATATA: The Spanish version of potato salad is different from the American version served at so many picnics and potlucks. Spanish potato salad can be served in two different ways.
- Ensaladilla (Potato Salad) is made with boiled potatoes, slices of hard boiled eggs, tuna, peas, red peppers, and mayonnaise. Olives can be added too.
- Papas Aliñadas are made with boiled potatoes, chopped eggs, tuna, olive oil, salt, and black pepper.

<u>FISH</u>: There are so many kinds of seafood in this region! Some are described previously, but if you visit the fish market you will want to bring a dictionary. Some of the best are *lubina* (sea bass), *dorada* (gilt-head bream), *urta* (rockfish), or *salmonetta* (red mullet). Bacalao (cod) is also common, but usually prepared with lots of salt. Be sure to ask for the fish *limpio*, so they will clean and gut is for you. Then, no matter what kind of fish it is, you can roast it whole for 20- 30 minutes with a little olive oil, salt, and herbs, and it will be an impressive delicious dish. Just watch out for bones when you are serving a whole fish. To serve, remove the head and peel back the skin on one side. Carefully remove the bones by scraping against them gently with a fork. Then turn the fish over and do the same on the other side. Whole fish is healthy, easy to cook, and worth a try. I hope you will venture to the market to enjoy a fresh catch!

URTA Á LA ROTEÑA (Rota's Local Specialty)

1 Whole Urta (Rockfish)
or other Whole Fish, weighing about ½ kilo (1 pound)
Salt
4 Tomatoes, Peeled and Chopped
2 Green Peppers, Seeded and Chopped
1 Onion, Finely Chopped
2 Cloves Garlic, Minced
½ cup Sherry
1/3 cup Olive Oil, divided

Rub the fish inside and out with salt, and sprinkle with some olive oil and all the sherry. Roast at 350° for 30 minutes, until fish is opaque white and flakes easily.
Meanwhile, heat the remaining of olive oil in a pan, over medium heat. Cook all the vegetables for 10-15 minutes, until tender. Serve the vegetables with the fish.

<u>CHEESE</u>: There are a variety of cheeses, both hard and soft, available in Spain. Some are made from cow's milk, especially in the north, but in the south it is more typical to find cheese made from goat's milk. Throughout the country, you can find the famous Manchego cheese, made from sheep's milk. It is formed into small circular wheels, and usually sold by the wedge. *Semicurado* (aged less than 13 weeks) is soft and has a mild flavor. *Curado* (aged up to 6 months) is firm and slightly salty because it is more aged. *Viejo* (aged over 6 months) is hard and very salty. Manchego is the typical cheese served on a sandwich or a restaurant cheese platter.

<u>CHOCOLATE Y CHURROS</u>: These are traditional foods found in bars or churros stands in the winter, or during any holiday. Churros are fried dough, not thick like funnel cake, but light and crispy, like a sweet French fry. They are typically prepared as sticks sprinkled with sugar, and served hot in a rolled piece of paper. They are ordered by the kilo, although a half kilo (1 pound) is enough for several people to share. The hot chocolate is extremely rich and thick—almost like hot pudding. You dip the churros into the chocolate and enjoy!

<u>COFFEE</u>: Coffee is popular in Spain—not just in the mornings, but as a late afternoon break, too. It is available at bars and restaurants throughout the day. The most common version is *café con leche*, coffee with milk. It is made with steamed milk in equal portion to the coffee, and usually served in a tall glass with one or two packets of sugar. Straight black coffee is *café solo*, served in small cups. *Café americano* is coffee with a shot of espresso.

SANGRIA AND TINTO DE VERANO: Sangria is a popular summer drink made of cheap red wine mixed with fresh fruit, juice, and ice. It is served by the pitcher, *una jarra*, or by the glass, *una copa*. When served at a bar or restaurant, it is usually fortified with strong liquor such as rum and/or brandy, so be careful how quickly you drink! Sangria is served at many restaurants, but the Spanish drink it for special events like parties, family barbeques, etc. *Tinto de verano*, which translates as 'red wine of summer' is a cheaper summer drink, more common for an everyday meal. It is like sangria, but without any fruit or added sugar, which is how the locals prefer it. *Tinto*, as it is usually called, is red wine with sparkling sweetener, like 7Up or lemonade. Very refreshing! It is not as potent as sangria, but still good. You can buy ready-mixed bottles of tinto at any local grocery store, either in original flavor or with lemon added.

TRADITIONAL SANGRIA RECIPE:

1 Bottle of Cheap Red Wine
Equal Quantity Of 7 Up, Sprite or Other Sparkling Lemon Drink
½ Cup of Liquor (usually Brandy)
A Peach, Apple, and an Orange, Chopped
¼- ½ Cup Sugar
Sprinkle of Cinnamon

Chop up fruit, then combine all ingredients in a large pitcher with plenty of ice. Allow flavors to mix and blend. Serve well chilled.

SHERRY: Rota is in the "Sherry Triangle" region of Spain, which is famous for the production of sherry wines. Sherry has a distinct flavor, which is an acquired taste. It has been made in this region for several thousand years, since before the Roman Empire! Of course the process was different then, but the region became known to the Romans because of the unique alcohol being produced here. The nearby town of Jerez (pronounced Hair-eth) means 'sherry'. There are a variety of sherries, ranging from light to dark, bitter to sweet.

Dry sherries are made from Palomino grapes, harvested at the beginning of September. The first pressing, from minimal pressure, is used to make the lighter Manzanilla and Fino sherries, which will ferment to 15% alcohol content. The 2nd pressing makes the richer Oloroso sherry, which is fermented to 17%. Sweet sherries are made from Moscatel and Pedro Ximenez grapes, which are dried in the sun. This raises the sugar content and gives a strong raisin-y flavor. Sweet sherries are only partially fermented, so they can maintain their sugar. Tintilla is a special sweet sherry made only in Rota, at the town's only remaining bodega, El Gato.

Sherry is aged differently from wine. It goes through biological aging, where yeast forms a solid layer called '*flor*,' or a floral veil, that protects the sherry from oxidization and interacts with the sherry. Lighter colored sherries have a lower alcohol content that allows the flor to remain intact. Darker color sherries have a higher alcohol content, which kills the flor and allows oxidization, giving them their darker color. The sherry is aged in huge oak barrels, called *botas*, which are not completely filled, and the valve on top is left open to let air in. To serve the sherry, a special instrument called a '*venencia*' is used. It is so slender that it will not disrupt the flor, but requires a skilled practiced hand to pour it into tiny sherry glasses. The server holds the *venencia* over their head, and then lets the sherry fall in a steady stream to land precisely in the glasses.

Bodegas are the buildings where sherry is aged, stored, and sold. Some are large and well-known, like Tio Peppe or Osborne. Others are quite small. But all have rows of barrels stacked in 2 or 3 layers, called a *solera*. During aging, the sherry is rotated from the top layer (the younger sherries) to the lower layers (older sherries), and mixed to achieve a balanced flavor. So sherry bottles do not generally have a particular age or year, since one bottle contains a variety of years. Some rare sherry is 20 years old or even 30 years old.

RESTAURANTS IN ROTA

There are numerous dining options in Rota, from small family-owned restaurants, to nightclubs, beachside bars, or ethnic food from countries around the world. The author has not personally been to every restaurant, and cannot account for changes in menus, ownership, or quality since publication. Many of the smaller restaurants offer similar menus of traditional Spanish fare, as described previously in this chapter. But some of the restaurants that are popular with Americans are reviewed below. Keep in mind that Spanish hours are 1-3 pm for lunch, and 8-11 pm for dinner, unless otherwise noted. Most restaurants are closed on Mondays. (Information was accurate at printing date, 2014).

BAR GOMEZ: This is one of the best locations for a traditional Spanish breakfast. They open early and serve giant *bocadillos* (sub sandwiches) covered with fried eggs, meat, cheese, tomatoes, and/or tortilla. Their smaller sandwiches are *guatangas*, served on a hot dog-sized roll. The menu is available until the afternoon. The bread is fresh and crusty, and all the other ingredients are fresh too. Since each sandwich is only 2 Euros, you'll probably pay more for your coffee and fresh-squeezed orange juice. It's a very small, casual bar located at Calle de Rubén Darío, 19 (near the giant hands circle). Street parking only.

BADULAQUE: This great restaurant is located on Rota's main boardwalk, with wonderful views of the beach. It is in the Plaza Jesús Nazareno, 5. Closed on Tuesdays. They offer somewhat traditional seafood and meat dishes, but with a modern flair. It's a great place to stop for tapas and get a sampling of several dishes at once. They also have an extensive wine selection. Prices are moderate to expensive. There are a few parking spaces on the plaza, but in summer plan to walk or take a cab. We usually park in the harbor (free in winter, fees in summer), then walk along the *paseo* for about 10 minutes until we reach it.

<u>100 MONTADITOS</u>: This is a fast-food chain that can be found throughout Spain. Here, it is in the Plaza Jesús Nazareno, across from Badulaque. A *montadito* is a small bun topped with meat, cheese, or seafood salad—like a small sandwich. They offer 100 different varieties on their menu. You fill out your order at the table, using the menu numbers, then turn it in at the counter. Plan to eat 2 or 3 different sandwiches if you are hungry, since each is only a few bites. The food is cheap quality, but offers a surprising variety of Spanish flavors, and it is served very quickly. This is also a great place to watch the boardwalk or the sunset throughout the summer season. Prices are inexpensive, and parking is limited. Wednesdays are 1 Euro day, where the entire menu is 1 Euro.

<u>PARRILLA LOS ARGENTINOS</u>: This is a small, but wonderful, restaurant in Rota loaded at Avda. Principes de España 74. It is one of the few restaurants open on a Monday, (closed Wednesdays) and also one of the few places to get a good steak. Parrilla means 'grill.' Their specialty is grilled Argentinian beef, and a half steak is delicious—lots of marbling, good flavor, and very tender. They boast other 'typical Argentinian dishes' but also have plenty of typical Spanish dishes, like fried cheese, grilled prawns, and grilled swordfish. Most dishes are served with a side of fries. Desserts include ice cream, and a flan that is very rich and smooth. The service here is at a slower pace. Prices range from average to high for a family meal. They have a child's menu. Expect to park on the street and walk a block or two, as the restaurant is located on a busy corner with no parking.

<u>LAS TINAJAS</u>: Located just outside Rota, on the road towards Chipiona (A-491), Las Tinajas is a great *parrilla venta* (which means roadside grill). Their wood-burning oven gives a great smoky flavor to kabobs, steaks, and grilled entrees. They have an excellent menu, good quality food, and delicious appetizers. This restaurant is child-friendly, since it has a kids' menu and a playground outside. It is popular for lunch or dinner. Prices moderate. Parking lot on site. You will see the restaurant on your left while driving on the A-491, but must drive past it to the next road and make a left off the highway there.

BAR LA FERIA: This tiny local bar, located in the old town of Rota on the pedestrian street Calle Mina 42, is a great place to taste some authentic Spanish food, and even see a small flamenco show! The shows are Friday evenings at 7:30 pm. The small stage only allows room for 1 guitarist, 1 singer, and 1 dancer, but the setting is intimate and allows you to rub elbows with locals. There is a fixed price menu including local favorites like jamón, fried peppers, garlic shrimp, or pork loin, with beverages included. Price for the dinner and show for two people is 50 Euros. It is located on a pedestrian street, so plan to walk or take a cab.

TAKIKO'S: This is an Asian restaurant that is a favorite with many base families. They are located on a small cul-de-sac off Avda. de la Diputation. Address is Torres de Banos 2 in Rota. They open at 6 pm for dinner. The cuisine is Japanese, Chinese, and Thai. They have a small selection of sushi dishes, a good selection of standard Chinese dishes and fried rice, and several spicy Thai items. The staff is Chinese and British, so they all speak English. This is one of the most relaxed and family friendly place we have visited! Instead of bread, the starter is shrimp rice cakes, which are very light and tasty. The portion sizes are reasonable on site and large for delivery. On site you can also choose from the buffet instead of ordering a la carte. The sushi is ok, not great. The dishes labeled *caliente* do indeed have a spicy punch. The chicken and shrimp fried rice sides are delicious, and large enough to share with the whole table. Prices are low to reasonable for a family, and they deliver to the base Rota gate. There is no parking on site, so expect to park on the street and walk a block or so.

LA DOLCE VITA: This tiny restaurant above Rota's port has some of the best Italian food in the area. Address is Calle Perez de Bedoya 13. Park near the port and walk up the stairs to reach it. The menu is limited to a handful of appetizers and pasta dishes, but everything is rich and extremely flavorful, made with very high quality fresh ingredients. Portions are small but very filling, and prices are moderate to high. Great date night destination, but reservations are necessary because of the limited space.

PIZZA Y PASTA: Avda de la Diputation 148. This is a great casual restaurant that is actually open for breakfast, lunch, and dinner. For breakfast and lunch they serve delicious sandwiches (*bocadillos*) on which you can order Manchego cheese, eggs, tomatoes, jamón, or deli sliced ham (*jamón York*). These come on fresh, soft bread rolls drizzled with olive oil. For dinner, they have a large selection of pizza toppings and fried dishes, as well as a small selection of pasta. The pizza is good—thin crust, minimal sauce, lots of cheese—but nothing special. Their Mexican dishes are tasty but not particularly authentic. Prices are low and reasonable for a family. The location is casual booths and tables, but they also have tables on the sidewalk with umbrellas and space heaters. They are located directly across from the natural park on the northwest edge of Rota. There is a small parking lot in front of the restaurant. They also deliver to the base.

SHANZA: There are several Shanza locations in Rota. The closest is by the circle with the giant hands: Avda. San Fernando, 56. Each of the three locations offers a tasty menu of Indian food: chicken, shrimp, or lamb curries, tikka, and tandoori dishes served over several kinds of rice, with assorted Nan bread accompaniments. You can request food that is moderate or spicy. Their prices are low to average, and the food is delicious and good quality. They are open for lunch and dinner every day, with early dinner hours several days per week. They deliver to base at the Rota gate.

LA ALMADRABA: Currently, this is the restaurant you will visit during ICR class. It is on the west edge of Rota, on the one-way road that runs parallel to the beach: Avda de la Diputation 140. The restaurant has a bar side which is more casual, and a dining side which has white tablecloths and china settings. They have plenty of starters such as cheese, lightly fried peppers, and prawns. The entree list is short, but delicious. The kebabs hang vertically in a special stand over your plate. They are tender and well-seasoned. The fish stew Rota style has large chunks of white rockfish in a typical tomato and green pepper stew. Mild, but satisfying flavors. There is no kids' menu, but there are croquettes and chicken nuggets. This is not a particularly family-friendly restaurant. The food prices range from moderate to high for a family. There is street parking available directly in front of the restaurant.

RESTAURANTS IN PUERTO

VENTA EL NENE: This tiny restaurant, located just outside the Puerto gate at the first traffic circle, is famous for its giant tortilla and "American style" breakfast. Their tortilla is the size of a large cake, and can feed a whole family. You can get a traditional one made with just potatoes, onions, and eggs, which is quite delicious, or you can have added flavors like peppers or meats. Prices are very reasonable. The American breakfast menu includes items like pancakes, waffles, omelets, or grits, which simply cannot be found at many other Spanish restaurants. They are open daily from 7 am- 9 pm.

PARRILLA BAILEY'S: A wonderful grill located not far from the Puerto gate, at Calle del Curricán, 2. They have a huge outdoor playground for the kids, and indoor or outdoor dining options. The menu includes delicious grilled fish, steak, or kebab options at moderate to high prices. Open for lunch on weekends, and dinner at 7 pm every day. Parking on site.

EL ULTIMO: This tiny bar is located just outside the Fuentabravia gate. They offer mainly tapas and drinks, which can be enjoyed in a comfortable setting of sofas and lounge chairs. Most hot dishes are simple fried foods, but very tasty and well prepared. They are open daily from 10 am- midnight, so it's a great place to meet for coffee or a light meal.

VENTA LA RUFANA: Located on the CA-603, 2.2 kilometers from base, just off a traffic circle across from Maxi Dia, this family-owned restaurant is a great place to get a taste of local Spanish cooking. It is sometimes referred to as "chicken in the dirt" because of their famous garlic chicken dish and their dirt parking lot. The homemade food includes delicious fish and meat dishes at moderate prices. They are open during Spanish hours only, and do NOT accept credit cards.

BAR JAMON: A fancy place for some high-quality Spanish cuisine in a relaxing setting. It is located at Glorieta Molino Platero, near the Puerto Feria grounds. The prices are high, but the food is designed to impress. There is live piano music performed on the weekends. Hours are Spanish, and there is parking on site.

CRÊFONDUE: A chain restaurant that serves both crêpes and fondue? Sounds like a perfect date night location! The one in Puerto Sherry overlooks the beach, and has amazing views of Cádiz and the sunset. It is located at Pueblo Marinero Local 100, but you will have to park at one end of the port or the other and walk the street along the beach until you come to the string of restaurants including a gin bar, sushi bar, Blanco Paloma, and then Crêfondue at the end. Parking in summer is very limited. The appetizers and desserts are amazing! Savory crêpes for a main course are average. Also offers sandwiches and salads. Prices are a little high, even compared to other restaurants on that street. Open daily from 10:30 am- Midnight, and reservations are recommended for dinner.

BLANCO PALOMA has two locations: one in Puerto Sherry, and one near the Feria grounds. The one in Puerto Sherry is right next to Crêfondue, described above, and has the same amazing ocean views. The other is located at Calle Paloma Zurita, 1. Both have the same extensive pizzeria menu, with a great selection of sandwiches, pizza, pasta dishes, salads, and appetizers. The food is always delicious, particularly salads and pastas, and the prices are reasonable. They are closed on Wednesdays, open during Spanish lunch and dinner through the week, and stay open from 1pm- midnight on weekends. The Puerto Sherry restaurant is a great location to take visitors for a good meal with a great view.

VENTA LA FERIA: This is THE place to go for paella in Puerto. They specialize in different paella dishes, and have a large number on the menu, ranging from meat to seafood to vegetarian paellas, with traditional yellow or even rare black rice, flavored with squid ink. Keep in mind that paella is prepared fresh, and takes at least 30 minutes to cook, so the wait can be long—but worth it. Paella is usually portioned to be shared with 2 or more people, so the table must agree on one dish. Average price is 20 Euros per person. From base, take the 491 past the Puerto Feria grounds, and take the exit after the Feria grounds to Carretera de Sanlúcar (A-2001). The restaurant is immediately on your left. Parking is available on site.

LITTLE ITALY: While the Italian food here is average quality pizza and pasta, the location is popular because it has an indoor play area for children, allowing adults to relax in the upscale ambiance. The menu has plenty of great salad, pasta, and pizza options, as well as a few meat dishes. Prices are moderate to high. They are open daily for lunch and dinner, during Spanish hours. The address is Carretera Sanlúcar, 4 (right next to Bamboo Sushi). Parking is available in the dirt lot right out front.

BAMBOO SUSHI: This is one of the best sushi restaurants in the area. They have high quality ingredients, and a menu that includes sushi, maki, rolls, and sashimi. Portions are small, so plan to order several items. Prices per roll start at 3 Euros and go up to 8 Euros for rainbow rolls. They are located at Carretera Sanlúcar, 4 (right next to Little Italy) and have parking available in front. Closed Monday, open for lunch and dinner during Spanish hours.

SHAMROCK: A new Irish bar and restaurant that has become a big hit with Americans and Spanish, not only because of its convenient location near the Puerto gate, but also because of the excellent menu and the personal attention from the chef owner. From the Puerto gate, go 'straight' through two traffic circles, and it will be on your left. The basic menu includes great fish and chips, hamburgers, and pub appetizers, while the daily specials feature a burger of the day and spicy dishes. Prices are moderate, and parking is available on site. Open for dinner weekdays, and from Noon on weekends.

EL SITIO DE VELÉZ: This is a great, modern Spanish restaurant in the downtown port area of Puerto. Delicious tapas, salads, entrées, and desserts, all served with a modern flair and accompanied by quality wines. The menu is prepared with traditional Spanish ingredients, but with a new twist of additional foods and flavors that make each dish unique. Prices are high, reflecting the upscale ingredients and presentation. It is located at Plaza Galeras Reales, 3 with parking a few blocks away. They open for dinner at 8 pm.

PART IV: TRAVEL

General Travel Information: Trains, Planes, Busses, and
    Lodging
Making Your European Bucket List
Travelling With Children
Kids' Field Trips
Outdoor Adventures
Day Trips:
    Arcos
    Baelo Claudia
    Cádiz
    Ceuta
    Chipiona
    El Portal (Horse Ranch)
    El Puerto De Santa Maria
    Gibraltar
    Jerez
    Medina Sidonia
    Ronda
    Rota
    Sanlucar Horse Races
    Sevilla
    Tangiers, Morocco
    Ubrique
    Vejer de la Frontera
    Zahara de la Sierra
Weekend Trips:
    Cordoba
    Granada
    Lisbon, Portugal
    Madrid
    Toledo

GENERAL TRAVEL INFORMATION

Traveling in Spain or around Europe may sound intimidating at first, but of course it is a popular activity for everyone stationed here in Rota. Just as there are numerous travel search engines in the United States, there are different websites useful for European travel. Many are either already in English, or can be translated by selecting that option on the page. Travel websites for trains, planes, busses, and lodging will be discussed on the following pages. Generally, the earlier you start your search, the better rates you will find. It is always more expensive to travel during holidays like Christmas or August, whereas the cheapest travel months are October and January.

If you don't want to do logistical planning yourself, MWR hosts trips throughout Spain and Europe, where they make all the airfare and hotel arrangements. But you can get much better rates if you do the research and make your own reservations. You can use the websites on the following pages to make reservations and plan a trip. The base Library has a good collection of travel guides to help you choose a destination. If you are unsure about making reservations yourself, you can always visit a local travel agent. There are several in Puerto and Rota that speak English and can get you the best rates without all the headaches. (Look for their ads in The Coastline newspaper).

When making any travel reservations, whether it is hotels, plane tickets, or train tickets, always get traveler's insurance. Military members can usually get the best rates from USAA, which offers different levels of travelers' insurance, often for as low as $20- $50. This can save you serious money on otherwise 'non-refundable' tickets if you have to make last-minute changes or cancellations, especially if the reason is military orders. Of course remember to take your tourist passport anytime you are crossing Spain's border. You should not need to show your no-fee passport for leisure travel. However, because the no-fee is stamped with the *entrada* stamp when you arrive in Rota, some people take both passports to avoid questions at customs.

TRAINS

Train travel is much easier and more convenient throughout Europe than it is in America. Trains run frequently, and usually arrive on time. Taking a train can save you time and money, depending on your destination and the number of people in your family. If you are travelling with children, a train ride could be more fun than a car ride, because they will have room to stretch out, walk around, or eat. Children under 4 usually ride free, but you will not have a seat reserved for them, so they may need to stay in your lap.

You must have a ticket before boarding the train, but it is usually possible to buy one just hours or days before you travel, without making a reservation. The Spanish train company is called RENFE. Train tickets can be purchased at the website www.Renfe.com/EN, which is already partially translated into English. Most of the discounts listed online are for young people or elderly, or those with official documentation from the Spanish government, which is usually unavailable to American citizens. In general, it is most affordable to purchase roundtrip tickets: *Ida y Vuelta*. Many Americans report problems having credit card payments accepted on the website, so you can also buy tickets at the kiosks of train stations in El Puerto de Santa Maria or Jerez. More discounts are available at the kiosks than online.

The AVE trains are high-speed trains that travel on limited routes. Fares are usually highest for these trains, but travel time to places like Barcelona, France, or Italy can be greatly reduced. There are slower local trains that travel from Cádiz to Sevilla or Madrid, with the closest stops at El Puerto de Santa Maria and Jerez. If you have family visiting from the States, they can fly into the Madrid airport, transfer to the Madrid train station, and take a train directly to El Puerto de Santa Maria. The tickets are still expensive, but can save money and time instead of taking a connecting flight.

If you are planning a lot of trips in a short amount of time, you can purchase a Spain pass. It is good for a certain number of journeys, but they must all occur within one month.

PLANES

Because Rota is located at the southwest corner of Spain, air travel is almost the only option when trying to reach another country (unless you are up for a very long car or train ride). The closest civilian airport to Rota is in Jerez, about 20 minutes from base. But this is a local airport, and most connections go through Sevilla or Madrid. Sevilla's airport is just over 1 hour from base, and Malaga is over 2 hours away. Usually, if family comes to visit from the States, they will be looking for flights to one of those airports. They can also land in Madrid and take a train all the way to Puerto, which is not always the cheapest option, but very convenient.

There are several good discount airlines in Europe. The most popular is RyanAir, and their website is www.RyanAir.com. This is a British airline with service to most European capitals and major cities. However, as a discount airline it often uses the less convenient airport, located farther away from a city center, so research the shuttle options in advance. Tickets can be extremely low at times, often starting at 20 Euros! But pay attention, because as a no-frill airline they will charge you extra fees for everything, from reserving an actual seat number, to checking a bag, to priority placement at the front of the line. RyanAir operates out of Sevilla, Malaga, and Madrid, but with limited destinations from each of those airports.

Another popular airline is Iberia, a Spanish company with international service. Their website is www.Iberia.com. They typically have flights out of Jerez, Sevilla, Malaga, or Madrid. They are much larger and serve most major European destinations, but some destinations are very expensive.

A good way to search all flight options simultaneously is with a search engine like www.SkyScanner.es, which gives you language and money options at the top of the page. You can type in destinations and compare which airline has the best option from which airports. You can also search dates for an entire week or an entire month at a time. Of course you can always use a travel agent, too. Air travel is usually most expensive during the months of December, July, and August, and cheapest during October and January.

SPACE A (SPACE AVAILABLE) TRAVEL

Naval Station Rota has its own airfield, and military flights depart regularly for the United States and locations across Europe and Asia. When there is space available on these flights, military personnel and their dependent family members who are stationed overseas are allowed to fly for FREE. From Rota, it is easy to travel Space A back to the East Coast airports like Dover Delaware, Charleston South Carolina, or Norfolk Virginia. From there, you can get another Space A flight, rent cars, or take civilian flights to your destination. In Europe, there are Space A flights to Ramstein Germany, Sigonella Italy, Souda Bay Crete, or Incirlik Turkey. The 'rotator' is a commercial airline with regular seats, snacks, and flight attendants. It travels between the East Coast and Rota several times per week. Other Space A flights are on military aircraft like a C5 or C17. These can sometimes be loud, cold, and uncomfortable, so plan to bring sweaters, blankets, earplugs, and even pillows. The good news is that kids can often stretch out on these planes and make a cozy bed space next to military equipment.

By following the websites (Facebook pages) for desired airports, you can see flights posted up to 3 days in advance. Start by getting a command-sponsored flight letter from the active duty member's command. You can then take it to the terminal on base, and they will explain the Space A process to you. Space A can be a great option for family emergencies requiring travel back to the States, but can be a little trickier to use for leisure vacation travel. First of all, military personnel must be on leave before they can check in for Space A travel. If flights are delayed (which happens often), the military member may have to waste several leave days waiting for the plane to depart. Also, there is a priority system to ensure that space is given first to those who need it most. Category I is for people travelling on military orders. Category II is for emergency travel. Leisure travel for a service member and family is Category III. Family members travelling without their service member (to visit the States for the summer, for example) are all the way down in Category V. So even though flights are announced as having space available, you never know how many people will be in categories ahead of you to claim all the seats. This means people often report to the air terminal several days in a row before finally making it onto a flight. Keep in mind that you will go through the same procedure to fly Space A on your return flight, so you may be delayed for days or weeks at your destination. To check in to a Space A flight, you can sign up on the website Takeahop.com and register for the airports you want to visit. Try to be flexible: even though you may want to visit family in a specific location, consider all military airports on the East Coast, and renting a car or paying for short flights to get to your end destination, since the Space A list to and from Norfolk fills up quickly. Then you need to arrive at the air terminal ahead of time, with your bags fully packed and ready to go, and the required paperwork. Once your name is selected, you are not typically permitted to leave the terminal and pack anything else. More information about paperwork, airport locations, and flight times can be found on the website http://www.amc.af.mil/amctravel/.

CITY PASSES AND BUSSES

Many large cities in Spain and throughout Europe offer package deals for tourists. They might be called 'Madrid Card' or 'Paris Visite,' but the general idea is that you purchase the Pass ticket for a flat rate, and then use it to enter common attractions and public transportation for free. The tickets let you skip some lines and can save you money... but they are usually priced so that you only see savings if you go to LOTS of museums and monuments. Typically, they are good for 1 or 2 days. So if you are planning a whirlwind tour of a major city with just you and your spouse, look into the City Pass. But if you are spending a leisurely week in the city with children, it is probably not a good investment.

Many cities also offer tours with a Hop-On Hop-Off Bus. This is an international company in major cities. Their website is http://www.hop-on-hop-off-bus.com. A big red double-decker bus makes a circular route of the city, passing by major attractions and historical sites. You can listen to the commentary on the headphones, or get off and explore a site. Tickets are more expensive than public city busses, but the ride is more convenient since you don't have to worry about changing lines, or looking up bus numbers and schedules. This can be a good option with children to save them some walking. But if you can get a good map of city bus routes, your kids will enjoy those too, and you will just pay a few Euros to ride.

LODGING

There are numerous ways to make hotel reservations, whether you make them in connection with your plane tickets, on your own, or through a travel agent. The website www.skyscanner.es can also be used to search and compare hotel options. If you make your own reservations, consider renting a room or apartment, fully furnished, from websites like www.flipkey.com or www.AirBnB.com. This will let you compare apartments at your destination, and make a selection based on location, number of bedrooms, or amenities. We have found it is usually cheaper for our family to rent an apartment than a large hotel room. The apartment gives us more bedrooms, and also has a full kitchen, so we can prepare our own meals and save money. These locations have reviews from other visitors, and you can benefit from meeting a local host and getting a more personal experience than you would get at a hotel. Just remember that apartments don't usually have the same amenities a hotel does, so be sure to confirm things like Internet access and air conditioning before you book.

As a military family, you can also benefit from military lodges and USO centers located across Europe. These are discounted hotels available only to military and DoD civilian families, located on small military bases throughout the world. Accommodations are simple, usually like a motel with two double beds per room, but the money saved can be significant for a family travelling to an expensive location. Some examples are the Navy Lodges and Gateway Inns in London England, Brussels Belgium, Ramstein Germany, Souda Bay Greece, Azores Portugal, Naples Italy, or Camp Darby in Tuscany Italy. For reservation information, visit www.dodlodging.com.

Finally, there are USO centers in several locations in Germany and Italy, which not only provide comfort areas in airports, but also can make lodging arrangements for military families and provide discounted tours and daytrip itineraries as well. To find out more about USO activities in Europe, visit http://www.uso.org/Centers/USO-Centers---Europe.aspx.

MAKING A EUROPEAN 'BUCKET LIST': EXPERIENCES MAY VARY

Many conversations on base begin with travel plans: "where have you been, where are you planning to go, what would you recommend in Rome, etc." Of course, most of us want to make the most of our European experience. However, it can be intimidating and overwhelming trying to decide how to visit so many glamorous places. And it can be easy to develop travel envy after seeing pictures from a friend's recent trips to Greece, Italy, Prague, AND Paris.

One way to combat travel envy and make travel plans that are best for your family is NOT to compare your experiences to others. Remember that every family stationed here has their own unique situation: some are only here for two years, others for four. We all have different family sizes and pay grades. Sometimes family visitors help pay for elaborate trips, while other people's families make them pay out of pocket. When deciding where to take your next trip, how can you sort through all the exotic opportunities and choose something that will be fun, meaningful, and affordable?

The first task is to PRIORITIZE WHAT IS IMPORTANT TO YOUR FAMILY. Travel is not just about seeing the world and checking off boxes in a guide book. It is ultimately about forming memories that will bring you closer to your travel companions. So do you want to travel with or without your children? Does your family enjoy history? Or do you prefer outdoor adventure? Do you like long car trips? Or prefer to remain in one place and explore? Have you always dreamed of visiting your ancestor's hometown? Depending on your answers, your ideal trip may be a wine-tasting tour, visiting Roman ruins, skiing in the Alps, driving across Tuscany, taking a Mediterranean cruise, or exploring a small town in Ireland. Choose the activities and locations that are most significant for your family. If your children are old enough, include them in the planning process, and ensure that each child gets to choose at least one destination or activity during the family vacation.

Next, CONSIDER YOUR BEST COUNTRY FIT. Some Americans adjust very well to life in Spain: they love the relaxed lifestyle, the long leisurely meals, the family atmosphere, and the abundant seafood. They would enjoy other Southern European cultures like Italy and Greece. Other people are naturally more suited to a

Northern European lifestyle. Germany, Austria, and Switzerland are the opposite of Spain. Things are very organized and timely, English is widely spoken, children should not be seen or heard, and of course there is plenty of hearty food and beer. When you visit a culture that you can relate to, it is an unforgettably enjoyable experience. When you spend time in a culture that doesn't make sense to you, you may go through the motions of being a tourist, but walk away a little confused and disappointed.

Then you need to SET A BUDGET. It doesn't have to be an exact dollar amount, but as you and your spouse plan future trips, you need to be on the same page financially. Some families are comfortable going into credit card debt for a once-in-a-lifetime experience. Others refuse to take trips they cannot pay for by saving in advance. The choice is yours, but you must make it with your spouse. Realistically, most military families can only afford 1 or 2 big 'international trips' (outside Spain) each year. Don't forget to factor food costs, attraction passes, museum fees, and local transportation costs into your overall trip budget. If you want to spend a week in Italy, you may be sacrificing the chance to spend a few 3-day weekends in Spain or Portugal. Do you prefer to have smaller shorter trips to look forward to throughout the year? Or would you rather save all your money and vacation days for one glorious summer adventure?

Don't forget to CONSIDER WEATHER AND SEASONS! While Spain is pleasantly comfortable all year long, most of Europe is rather cold and dreary in the winter months. It can be nice to visit the mountains and get postcard-like views during Christmas, but the bitter cold and the icy conditions can make sight-seeing a little challenging. On the other hand, the summer months are peak tourist season throughout Europe, so you will have to deal with long lines and higher prices. Research your chosen country ahead of time and determine when it makes the most sense for you to visit.

Finally, DON'T NEGLECT SPAIN! Spain has glorious beaches, ancient castles, non-stop fiestas, and some of the best cuisine in the world. So take the time to enjoy Spain with day-trips to local towns, weekend trips to Madrid, Toledo, Barcelona, or Tenerife, and get involved in unique cultural opportunities like bull fights and fútbol matches. You won't regret your local adventures, and they can help you make memories and save money while dreaming of those destinations farther out of reach.

TRAVELING WITH CHILDREN

Some people with young children would never consider traveling in another country. Ours are currently 6, 4, and 2, and 0. We are brave (or crazy) enough to try everything. If you are physically and mentally prepared, traveling with children can be enjoyable for everyone. With very young children, you have to prepare a light itinerary. Start with local day trips to get your children used to the idea of exploring new cities. Soon they will learn the routine: long drive, walk around a bit, lunch, walk some more, drive home. When you are ready to plan weekend trips farther away, keep the daytrip routine in mind. Cities that are listed as a great 'day trip' from the main tourist route are often more relaxing for us as a weekend trip. With children you won't be able to do or see as much as you would with adults, because you need to walk slower, and make frequent stops for snacks, bathrooms, and nose wiping. But children under 5 get free admission to most sites, and they travel for free on public transportation, so adventures can be fun and inexpensive.

WHAT TO DO: Try to plan only 1-2 major activities per day. If your kids are old enough, involve them in the planning. Our kids have enjoyed historic sites like castles, churches, and history museums. We make up games, pretending to be knights, princesses, or adventurers. I research ahead of time to get facts and history from guidebooks, which I can translate into kid-friendly stories during dull moments. When visiting a museum, we draw pictures of things they might see, and then whoever spots a palm tree, water, or an elephant, gets to cross it off. After a 'boring' visit to a cathedral, we get some ice cream or take a break at a playground. Whenever possible, avoid long lines by ordering your tickets in advance.

WHERE TO STAY: We prefer to rent a fully-furnished apartment near the city's historic center, which is often the same price (and much more comfortable!) than a hotel room. You can find these at websites like AirBnB.com or www.flipkey.com. A central location will limit your walking and travel time, so you can return throughout the day. Apartments have a kitchen to prepare meals, and separate bedrooms for the kids. We have had a wonderful time meeting and chatting with local hosts. The only downside is that you may not get the quality of amenities you would in a hotel, such as central heating and air conditioning, so double-check before you make a reservation.

GETTING AROUND: We use a baby backpack to carry the youngest, but the other 3 have to walk or take brief rests in a stroller, so they can only do a few hours of walking total per day. Strollers are inconvenient on steep hills or cobblestone streets, so plan on the kids walking most of the time. Luckily, public transportation like metro or busses are very exciting to them, and much cheaper than taxis.

HOW TO GET THERE: For most weekend trips, we choose locations we can drive to in a day. If you drive, you can bring many more comforts with you. I pack food, so we can eat in the car when there are no rest stops. Be sure to bring a 1st Aid kit and children's medicine. We pack baby equipment, including diapers, strollers and the backpack carrier, but the apartment host provides a high chair and crib. However, there are lots of hidden costs of driving: gas is twice as expensive in Europe, you will have to pay for parking during your stay, and there are numerous tolls on the roads (and if you have a large car like a minivan, you will pay class 2 tolls, which are double the class 1 rates). Trains are very comfortable and exciting for children. Youth age 4 and under travel for free. Air travel is the most expensive and frustrating with children. Pack carefully, because discount airlines like RyanAir are very strict about luggage size and weight, and will charge you hefty fees if you go over. You can check a stroller or baby car seat with your luggage, but make sure you have filled out this request in advance so you won't be charged extra. Allow plenty of time to get to an airport and find your gate, and when making reservations be careful of layover times. A 2-hour layover in the Madrid airport sounds like a long time, but it is actually the *minimum* amount of layover time you will need when transferring from the local to the international (non EU country) terminals with children. When you are rushed and stressed, your kids will be too.

KNOW WHEN TO QUIT: Keep an open mind, be flexible, and remember that a family trip is about the journey, not the destinations. When our son got feverish in Lisbon, we had to scratch "the essential day trip" because we would just be dragging exhausted children along. Instead we spent a relaxing and surprisingly fun day at the apartment, and that is more important than any castle or tourist site. So try to laugh at mistakes and the 'learning experiences,' and enjoy your family moments in Europe!

KIDS' FIELD TRIPS

ZOO IN JEREZ: The Jerez zoo is a good sized location, with a variety of exotic animals like lions, tigers, giraffes, monkeys, elephants, and zebra, as well as plenty of birds and reptiles. It is not a world-famous zoo, but is the perfect size for young children, since they can see almost everything within a few hours, have lunch, go on a train ride, and still make it home for an afternoon nap. The website is: http://www.zoobotanicojerez.com/. In summer they are open daily from 10 am- 7 pm. From September to May, they are closed Mondays, and close early other days at 6 pm. Adult admission is about 9 Euros, child admission is 6 Euros, and children 2 and under are free. There is also a tourist train that takes you through the zoo and costs an additional 2 Euros per person. You can purchase annual passes for individuals or families that are a good discount if you plan to make multiple visits (family pass for parents and all children is 43 Euros). The zoo entrance is located on Calle Madreselva in Jerez, and has a large parking lot. GPS coordinates: 36°41'20.8"N 6°09'00.8"W. There is a gift shop, snack bars, and a restaurant on site, but packing a picnic lunch is recommended.
Note: if you are interested in a larger zoo, the Selwo Aventura near Estepona and Malaga is a Safari park. Their website is: http://www.selwo.es/en.

AQUALANDIA: A water park located just off base, this location is better for older children, because it has a variety of huge water slides, rapids, wave pool, and other water activities. There is a small area with water fountains and miniature slides for younger children. They are open from June-September from 11 am- 6 pm. Tickets are cheaper on their website (in English!): http://www.aqualand.es/bahiadeCádiz/ but also available on site. Prices are around 20 Euros per adult, and 15 Euros per child, 8 Euros for toddlers, and babies free. There are also family packages and season discounts available. From the Puerto gate, take the A-4 towards Jerez to exit 646 (just a few minutes down the road), and you will see the water park on your left at the traffic circle. GPS coordinates: 36°37'57.7"N 6°11'48.6"W.

DIVERTILANDIA: Located in Rota, this is an indoor playground with a ball pit, slides, and climbing area. It is designed for young children age 8 and under, and is popular for winter birthday parties or rainy day play dates. They offer food and beverages in their birthday party packages. They are closed Mondays, and open from 4:30- 9:00 pm other days. They are located at the edge of Rota in the industrial area, on Calle Madrigal de las Altas Torres.

EL BUCARITO: This farm is located just behind the base, off the A-491. They raise goats and pigs, and make their own line of cheese, jamón, jams, and honey to sell in the local area. Tours can be arranged for groups over 10 people at a rate of 14.50 Euros per person. (Additional charge for an English translator). It lasts from 9 am-2 pm, and includes a breakfast of toasts and toppings, a tour of the farm, and a tasting of all products. Kids will get to make their own cheese to take home, and get up close and personal with the hawks and birds of prey. Their website is http://www.elbucarito.es/.

BEE FARM IN JEREZ: El Museo de la Miel (Honey Museum), located on the farming estate Miel Rancho Cortesano is an interesting field trip for school-age children. The CDC and SAC programs on base usually offer a trip here during the year. Children can don beekeeper uniforms, get up close with the bees, and learn all about the process of making honey. They can also do crafts like make a beeswax candle or bring their own jar of honey home. Tour activity, length, and cost depend on group size, ages, and interests. The farm is located just outside Jerez, on Carretera de Jerez-Cortes. GPS coordinates: 36°39'35.3"N 6°00'48.7"W. Their website is http://www.ranchocortesano.net/index.php.

AQUARIUM IN SEVILLA: A new site opened in Fall 2014, the Acuario de Sevilla has one of the largest tanks in Spain or Portugal. Prices are 15 Euros per adult, 10 Euros per child (children under 4 free). Discounts available for families or groups. Website is http://www.acuariosevilla.es/. Address is Avda. Santiago Montoto, Sevilla.

CROCODILE FARM: An unusual opportunity for anyone who loves reptiles is the Granja de Crocodrilos Kariba in El Portal, on the way to Jerez. You can watch the animals being fed, and even see nests of babies. They are usually open to the public in the evenings, during feeding time. Address is CA-3113 11510 Puerto Real. GPS Coordinates: 36°33'10.3"N 6°08'04.9"W. (It is currently closed for renovations, but plans to reopen the summer of 2015). See their website for updated info: http://www.cocodrilosjerez.com/html.

LAS MARIAS HORSE FARM: This equestrian center in Puerto offers riding lessons, field trips, and birthday parties for children. They offer rides on the beach, private or group instruction, and a range of games and activities to allow children to ride on horses, carriages, and play games during a party. Prices for lessons or parties are usually 10 Euros per child. Website is www.centrolasmarias.com.

PRINCELANDIA: For girls of any age, this is a great location for a party or an afternoon of pampering. The staff will style hair, do face painting, and give manicures and pedicures to party participants. Then girls can choose from a huge section of dress-ups and accessories, and perform a modelling session on the catwalk. The store is located on the 2nd level of the Centro Commercial Bahia Mar in Puerto. Website is www.princelandia.com.

LA CIUDAD DE LOS NIÑOS Y LAS NIÑAS: This giant park in Jerez is a huge outdoor play area for older and younger children. Access to the general park area is free, but for 3 Euros, kids can enjoy some of the special attractions: a giant trampoline, a zip line, and a huge climbing area. They also offer birthday party packages, since you cannot bring in outside food and drink. It is open from 4-8 pm Monday- Friday, and 11 am-8 pm on weekends and holidays. Website is http://www.venalaciudad.com/. The park is located in Jerez on Avenida de Arcos de la Frontera. GPS coordinates: 36°41'32.9"N 6°06'18.4"W.

LASER TAG AND GO KARTING: Both these activities are available at two different areas of the Luz shopping center in Jerez. The Karting Racing is an indoor go kart track that offers high speeds at moderate-high prices. They are open daily from 11 am- midnight, and offer package deals for groups or birthday parties. Website is http://racingdakartjerez.es/. Laser Space is a large indoor laser tag court, located in the same shopping center. They have multiple activities to choose from, for children ages 6 and up, including several laser courts, Nerf battle options, and indoor climbing walls. They accommodate groups for birthdays or other events. Prices depend on activities selected, and promotions are available on their website: http://www.laserspace.es/jerez/.
GPS coordinates: 36°41'39.0"N 6°09'33.0"W.

ISLA MAGICA: Located in Sevilla, this is the closest amusement park. It has roller coasters, rides, shows, and water areas all with different themes, such as pirates, Aztec city of gold, Medieval adventure, jungle, etc. There is also a new water park with huge slides and wave areas. Full-day child tickets are about 20 Euros, and adult tickets are 30 Euros, with half-day, package deals, and group discounts available. Hours vary depending on the month, but they are primarily open from May through September, from about 11 am- 11 pm. Their website is http://www.islamagica.es/. Address is Pabellón de España - Isla de la Cartuja, 41092, Sevilla.

DOLPHIN AND WHALE WATCHING IN TARIFA: There are several different breeds of dolphins and whales that live in and migrate through the Strait of Gibraltar. You can see these animals by going on a tour boat from the seaside town of Tarifa. There are several different companies who offer the trips throughout the spring and summer months. Prices and boat sizes vary, from yachts to rigid inflatables. In 2014, a 2-hour boat ride to see whales and dolphins was 30 Euros per adult, 10-20 Euros for children. A 3-hour boat ride to see killer whales is only available in July and August, and slightly more per person. One website, available in English, is: http://www.whalewatchtarifa.net/eng/index.html.

OUTDOOR ADVENTURES

Southern Spain is sunny and beautiful for most of the year, so it is an ideal location for enjoying outdoor sports and activities. Here are some of the popular options for enjoying the outdoors around base.

BIKING: For recreational riding, check out the Costa Ballena park, or ride along the Puerto paseo (boardwalk) to the Valdegrana Parque natural. When biking in pedestrian areas, use the markers in the sidewalk to keep on the bike path. The roads around base are relatively flat, and commonly used for road bikes. There are some riding clubs and teams in the area. A publication of Mountain Bike trails is available through the Cádiz Office of Tourism website: http://www.Cádizturismo.com/publicaciones/rutas-en-btt-por-la-provincia-de-Cádiz.

HORSEBACK RIDING: There are several stables and ranches in the area that offer horseback riding, whether it is lessons, birthday parties for children, or sunset rides on the beach for adults. Check out Las Marias Equestrian Center in Puerto (info on p. 144) or Los Caireeles in Rota.

HIKING: There are tons of beautiful nature trails and hiking opportunities not far from the base. There are several books written about hiking opportunities in this region. Look online or in the NEX bookstore. Driving 1 hour toward the mountains will bring you to Sierra de Grazelema Park, near Zahara de la Sierra. This natural park has a huge lake, and offers a variety of watersports, hiking trails, and even a ropes course. You can camp overnight, or just visit for a day. Detailed descriptions of routes and maps of hikes throughout the Sierra de Grazelema mountains are available in Spanish at: https://sites.google.com/site/senderismotercertiempo/Home.
You can also download hiking guides for the region's Natural Parks (in English) from the Cádiz Office of Tourism: http://www.Cádizturismo.com/publicaciones/guia-de-ser.

BIRD WATCHING: Spain is located on the migration route between Europe and Africa, so this is a birdwatcher's paradise. Some of the best opportunities are in Doñana Natural Park, across the river from Sanlúcar de Barremeda. However, the park is protected and can only be visited with a guide. You can arrange to have a guided tour on foot, by bike, or on one of their river cruises. For more information, see their website:
http://www.discoveringdonana.com/index.htm.

WIND SURFING OR KITE SURFING: This water sport is most popular in Tarifa, which is possibly the wind surfing capital of the world because it is located on the point where the Atlantic meets the Mediterranean, and it is constantly windy there. It is an exciting sport to watch, or you can take lessons locally in Rota or Costa Ballena.

SKIING: The only place in Southern Spain that has natural snow in winter is the mountains, particularly the Sierra Nevada range around Granada. There is a ski resort with beginner slopes and lessons, and a place nearby to rent sleds for children (sleds are not allowed on the ski slopes, but can be used in other areas). Cheaper accommodations are available in the small towns around Granada, but make sure you have a vehicle that can handle snowy roads! MWR usually arranges a ski trip in January, so contact them for updated info on the best locations.

DAY TRIPS

The following section gives you some information about the towns that are close to the Naval Station, and up to 2 hours away. These are great places to take visiting guests to give them some exposure to Spanish culture and see some unique sites that cannot be found in the States. (Cities are listed alphabetically). They are also fun trips for a family to spend a day together, so get out and explore and have some adventures!

THINGS TO PACK ON A DAY TRIP:

- Camera—fully charged, and with space for new photos!
- Map and/or GPS
- Cell Phone, fully charged
- Tickets, if you purchased any in advance
- Euro Cash (for Parking, Admission fees, Lunch)
- Sunscreen
- Sunglasses
- Water bottle
- Snacks
- Jacket
- Umbrella
- Spanish Dictionary, or translator app
- This guidebook ☺
- Stroller or baby backpack, plenty of diapers, baby wipes, and extra clothes for children

ARCOS

In the mountains North and East of here, throughout Southern Spain, are numerous small villages. These white-washed quaint towns perched on cliffs and mountaintops are known as *Pueblos Blancos*, or white villages. A well-known white village, just 40 minutes from Rota, is the town of Arcos. Arcos de la Frontera is named for its arches, and for its location at the frontier of the war against the Moors. The arches were built throughout the city and to support the town's two main churches, Santa Maria de la Asunción and San Pedro. The two churches, both built in the 16th centuries, had such a strong feud that the Pope had to become involved and declare Santa Maria as the main church of the city. The oldest portion of Arcos is perched on a cliff at the top of the mountain. The streets have remained unchanged since the Middle Ages, so they are extremely narrow. There IS a parking lot at the top of the city, in the main plaza, but it is not recommended, since you will be literally scraping paint from your car onto some of the city walls to get there. Instead, use the parking garage at the lower edge of the city. GPS Coordinates: 36°45'03.7"N 5°48'48.5"W. There is also a large dirt parking lot free to the public, but if you park there, you have to hike up several hundred steps to get into the city. GPS coordinates: 36°44'59.8"N 5°48'54.0"W.

If you walk uphill from the wide modern streets to the more narrow ancient streets, you will find the highest point of the town at the main plaza, which is flanked by the Church of Santa Maria and the Parador. There is a *mirador* (overlook point) where you can see the steep cliff on which the city is built. You can look down at the Guadalete River, and out across the plain at the miles of farmland that surround the city. It is extremely windy up there, but the views are amazing! The Church of Santa Maria was built in the 16th century, on the site of a former mosque (typical in this region that was run by the Moors and then overtaken by Christians). The tower was modeled off the bell tower—the *Giralda*—in Sevilla. Unfortunately, the residents of Arcos ran out of funds before they could finish it. But the *azulete* tiles are still beautiful. This church stands at the town's main plaza, which has the mirador at one end and the Parador at the other. A Parador is a state-owned hotel built at a historical site. You can spend the night (if you want to pay the high rates!) or enjoy a meal with reasonable prices and great views. There are more than 80 Paradors throughout Spain, and this one is worth a visit for the cliff-side views and delicious food.

Arcos is also famous for its running of the bulls, which occurs every year on Easter. There are only a few cities in Spain that still hold a running of the bulls, and Arcos is one of them. With its steep and narrow streets, this is quite an event! One or two bulls are released into the streets, and stampede through the main portion of the town. Military personnel are not permitted to run with the bulls, but may be spectators on the side streets.

Another reason to visit Arcos is because of the confections made by a unique group of nuns. The *Convento de las Mercedarias Descalez* is a cloistered order of nuns who do not leave their convent or receive visitors. However, to sell their delicious cookies they have a rotating screened window, through which you can place an order. You put your money on the counter, and it rotates around with a box of cookies. You can only buy them by the box, and the cost is 5 Euros, but they are delicious. Flavors include chocolate, almond, or sugar. The convent is on Calle Escribanos, a major street between the two main city churches, so a walking tour will lead you past it.

Arcos is the town that hosts a living Nativity every year before Christmas. The entire town is transformed into a scene from ancient Bethlehem, and the streets are filled with animals and people in costume, enacting scenes with Roman soldiers, Jewish peasants, and of course the Holy Family and the Three Kings. Year-round, there is a tiny museum called Belén (meaning Nativity). This is a single large room filled with miniature dioramas of the events surrounding Jesus's birth. There is a scene with shepherds in the fields, the kings with their camels, Mary and Joseph arriving in Bethlehem, and the birth in the stable. Each scene is filled with amusing figures and details that children will love. The lights are programmed to change every few minutes to show each scene in sunset, night, and morning. The visit is FREE, but a donation is encouraged to upkeep the maintenance. It is located near the convent, on the way to San Pedro church.

Arcos is a delightful town that is certainly worth a return visit. It is a great place to take visitors so they can experience one of the *pueblos blancos* without traveling all day.

BAELO CLAUDIA (ROMAN RUINS)

This is a wonderful day trip for history lovers, visitors, and even young children. Spain was once part of the Roman Empire. Some of the oldest cities in this area were first settled by Phoenicians, then later rebuilt by the Romans. Southeast of Rota is the most complete Roman town excavated on the Iberian Peninsula: Baelo Claudia. This site is still being excavated, but the major portions of the city have been restored, including the Basilica and Forum, Theater, Temple of Isis, baths, and fish drying buildings.

Baelo Claudia is located on the coast, just southeast of Tarifa, in the small town of Bolonia. This coast is always windy, so bring a jacket. We located Bolonia easily with our GPS, then there were signs leading to the historical site. It was about one and a half hours from base. There is free parking onsite, and admission to the site is also free for EU residents. Simply show your EU drivers' license as identification, and save the 5 Euros adults typically would pay.

Visitors will first enter a small museum, where there are displays and videos in English and Spanish explaining a lot about the site and how objects are recovered, cleaned, and restored. The museum is basically two large rooms on one floor, and has artifacts such as a tall marble column, a headless goddess statue, several Roman coins, and actual Roman plumbing. Baelo Claudia got its name from Emperor Claudius, who ruled from 10 BC- 53 AD, and granted the city the distinction of *municipium*—a title affecting the way local inhabitants became Roman citizens. The city was destroyed by an earthquake in the 2nd century AD, and abandoned by the 6th century.

Visitors can then go outside and walk through the ancient city. Even though it was on the outskirts of the Roman Empire, Baelo Claudia was laid out exactly the same way as every Roman town, with all the same amenities you would find in a similar town in Italy during that time. The entire city was surrounded by a wall, parts of which have been reconstructed to stand about five feet tall. There were originally three aqueducts, which once stretched about 5 km, and brought fresh water to this coastal city. A small portion of one aqueduct remains. Most of the rocks on the site were hauled from a nearby mountain, but some are harvested coral. All the rocks were carefully cut and placed with Roman attention to detail.

You enter the site through the city's West Gate, and walk on the ancient cobblestone streets. In some areas, wide modern gravel avenues make the ruins easy to explore. There are informational signs in English and Spanish at the major parts of the town. The ruins are right next to the beach, so there is a gorgeous ocean view. On a clear day, you can see the coast of Africa (Morocco)! Baelo Claudia was an important Roman harbor because it was used to trade with Africa.

The town was famous for salted tuna and a fermented fish paste called *garum,* which was exported throughout the Roman Empire. Tuna was a dietary staple in Roman times, and is still popular in Andalusia. The Romans invented the process of catching tuna in *almadraba* nets, which is a style of netting still used in the region. The city's harbor and fish-salting areas have been excavated, and you can view the square holes used as salting vats for preserving the fish.

Like most Roman cities, Baelo Claudia had an elaborate bath house, which has been excavated and partially restored. There were four major areas: a cold room for bathing, a hot room (sauna), a shallow pool for splashing, and a court for exercise. There are stone 'pipes' underneath the sauna floor, which were used to bring in hot water and control the temperature. Bathing was a big part of Roman culture, and most citizens went to the bath house every afternoon.

The central focus of the site is the pillars of the Basilica and the open Forum behind them. They are located at the center of town, at the intersection of the two main streets. This is true for all Roman towns, which were all laid out the same way. The word *'Basilica'* does not mean church. It was the government center. The statue in the center is Emperor Trajan. He followed Claudius, from 54- 117 AD, so his statue was in the city at its peak. The columns of the Basilica have been restored, so it is easy to visualize. The streets around the Basilica were the market area, but they are still being excavated.

The major focal point at the north of the city is the amphitheater. The building is restored, and resembles a modern music hall. It was not a Coliseum for sports; rather, a theater with a stage and an orchestra pit for musicians, and a curved seating area built into the natural slope of the hill. Visitors can walk through one of the entrances and stand on a platform looking over the structure.

After spending a few hours at Baelo Claudia, visit one of the beach restaurants next to the site for a lunch with gorgeous beach views. Or continue to the nearby town of Vejer, described on p. 184.

CÁDIZ

This historical city is world-famous for the annual Carnaval celebration in February or March that makes the city vibrant with crazy costumes, singing performances, and crowds of celebrators. It is a gorgeous city worth visiting any time of year. Cádiz is built on a small peninsula, across the bay from Rota. It is one of the oldest continuously-inhabited cities in Europe—originally founded 3,000 years ago! It was taken over by the Phoenicians, Greeks, Carthaginians, Romans, then the Moors, and finally the Spanish. According to legend, Hercules founded the city of Gadira (Greek name of Cádiz) approximately 80 years after the Trojan War, around 1104 B.C. The Phoenicians called the city Gadir. Then the Romans settled the city and called it Gades. It became a thriving naval port for exporting olive oil and wine. Roman control lasted from about 500 B.C. until 500 A.D. After the Romans, the Visigoths, Moors, and eventually the Catholic Spanish inhabited the city. The current name Cádiz is derived from the Arabic name, Qadis, meaning 'walled city.'

During Spain's age of exploration, Cádiz was an important port. Columbus sailed from Cádiz for his 2nd and 4th voyages. It was the harbor for the Spanish Armada, and in 1587 the Englishman Sir Francis Drake led a surprise raid on Cádiz that destroyed about 30 Spanish ships. This delayed the sailing of the Armada, and influenced their eventual defeat. In the 18th century, when the Guadalquivir river become silted and less traversal, all the New World trade that was flowing through Sevilla was transferred to Cádiz. This was the city's golden age. If you wander through some of the *barrios* (neighborhoods), you will notice that many houses were constructed during that period. The city has a classy, romantic, 18th century vibe.

The history of this rich city is best appreciated by walking. The city is not large, and since it is surrounded on three sides by water, it is easy to keep your orientation, even on the narrow winding streets. Cádiz is full of interesting buildings that are built upon layers of other civilizations. There are several ways to get to Cádiz from Rota. You can take a ferry from Rota or Puerto, which only takes half an hour and costs about 2 Euros per person. Purchase tickets and board the ferry by walking to the end of the long pier in Rota's port. It is slightly cheaper and more convenient from Puerto's port, because the ferry runs more frequently there. If you drive to Cádiz, there is public parking near the port, underneath the Plaza San Antonio, or in several other underground garages along the northern and western edges of the city. The city of Cádiz has made walking tours easy by painting colored lines on the pavement to guide tourists to major landmarks. In some areas the lines are faded or the sidewalk is under construction, so it is best to stop by a tourist office and pick up a free map or walking guide first. There is one tourist office near the Port at Paseo de Canalejas, and another on the Playa de la Caleta near the castle of Santa Catalina.

The ferry schedule from Puerto or Rota to Cadiz is available here:
http://www.cmtbc.es/catamaran.php

Days are in Spanish, with F for Festivals (holidays), but times are easy to read. Cadiz's port is called 'Pz. Sevilla.'

If you come by ferry, you can easily walk the Green route, "The Medieval District," which highlights the Cathedral, the Roman Theater ruins, some of the city's oldest churches, and the ancient city walls. The Puerta de Tierra is the former city gate, which still stands and allows lanes of traffic to pass through. The Cathedral is one of Cádiz's most interesting landmarks. Constructed from the 18th-19th centuries, it is a mixture of architectural styles ranging from rococo to baroque to neoclassical. Unfortunately, the interior is now marred by nets permanently suspended from the ceiling to catch falling plaster.

The Purple route, "Shippers to the Indies," takes you past the homes and churches of the city's former wealthiest citizens, and up the Tavira tower, which offers panoramic views of the whole city. The church of Our Lady of El Rosario houses the large statue of the city's patron saint, and the nearby rococo style church of San Juan de Dios is small but gorgeous. The Purple route will take you past the Cádiz Museum in Plaza de Mina, one of the best history museums in this area. Admission is usually 2.50 Euros, but is FREE to EU citizens, or anyone with an EU driver's license. The museum gives great insight into the 3,000 year long history of this city. It is organized chronologically. Most of the remnants of the Phoenicians are funerary. Statues and artifacts from the Roman city of Baelo

Claudia are housed here. The upper level of the museum has a small collection of huge paintings and religious artwork.

If you have comfortable walking shoes, you can explore the Orange route, "Castles and Bastions" which extends along the city's perimeter. It provides gorgeous ocean views, a stroll through the formal Genoves Park, and the chance to explore the Castillo Santa Catalina and Cádiz's world-famous beach, the Playa de la Caleta. The Castillo is a star-shaped fort built in the 1690's to defend the Northern side of Cádiz. You can walk along the castle walls, and explore each tiny guard tower on the points of the fort. The castle and beach appear in one of the James Bond movies, *Die Another Day.* In the scene where Halle Berry comes out of the water and joins Bond for a mojito, they are supposed to be in Havana, Cuba, but the scene was filmed here! You can see the fort in the background.

The Blue route, "Cádiz Constitution," highlights the Plaza d'España with the Constitution monument, and the city's most modern squares and churches. This tour follows the route of the civic procession that proclaimed the Constitution in 1812. When Napoleon Bonaparte placed his brother on the Spanish throne, Cádiz was one of the few cities to withstand his rule during the "Peninsula War." It was in Cádiz that the Constitution of 1812 was passed, so for a brief period Cádiz was the capital of Spain. The monument to the Constitution is on the Northern side of the city, and is a very impressive memorial with a perpetual flame, and an empty chair surrounded by allegorical figures. In 1820, the *Gaditanos* (people of Cádiz) revolted to secure the Constitution's renewal. Their revolt spread across the country, becoming the Spanish Civil War.

Cádiz is gorgeous in the sunny summer, but also very festive and exciting around Christmas. And of course it has non-stop celebrations for Carnaval in February. It's a great city to enjoy pastries and culinary delights from any *panaderia* or *pasteleria*, and has numerous wonderful tapas bars and restaurants. One unique location to mention: Café Royalty is a lavish restaurant carefully restored to its 1912 splendor. Located at Plaza de la Candelaria, this Romantic period café is lavishly decorated with gilded scrollwork, large mirrors, and numerous details from the early 1900's. It's a gorgeous and unique environment to soak up the historical surroundings of this splendid city.

CEUTA (SPANISH AFRICA)

Spain owns several small territories and cities off the mainland. One of the more interesting in Ceuta, an autonomous city owned by Spain, but located across the strait of Gibraltar on the African continent, adjacent to Morocco. You can take a ferry from Algeciras, Spain (near Gibraltar) to Ceuta. Algeciras is 1.5 hours from Rota. The crossing takes about 1 hour each way, and costs about 70 Euros roundtrip (2014 prices).

Ceuta is a small city, only 7 square miles. It has a mixed population of Christians and Muslims, but it is still Spain, so the official language is Spanish and the currency is the Euro. The city was established as a Roman port, then taken over by Visigoths, then the Christians of the Byzantine Empire. In the 9th Century, it was rebuilt under Moorish rule. In the 1400's, it was captured by the Portuguese king (before Portugal was an independent country). Over the years, so many Spanish citizens came to Ceuta that the city maintained allegiance to Spain during the war with Portugal, and was awarded to Spain after the war. However, Ceuta retained the Portuguese coat of arms on its city flag.

Although it is on the African coast, Ceuta maintains a Spanish style in its architecture. It looks very much like Cádiz. The cathedral is yellow and white, built in the neoclassical and baroque style of the 17th century. The Royal Walls of the old medieval fort—which you can enter and climb onto—are similar to the star shape of the Cádiz castle. You can visit the archaeological excavation of a Christian basilica and necropolis from the 4th century. There is also a small museum, El Revellín, which has archaeology, history, and art exhibits. The Mediterranean Maritime park is a modern park with a recreated castle in the center, and several lakes and gardens. Or you can just walk along the harbor/waterfront area and enjoy the gorgeous views! There are plenty of restaurants and cafés catering to tourists, where you can enjoy Spanish tapas, Moroccan tagine, or even McDonald's.

From Ceuta, you can cross the international border into Morocco to visit towns like Fez. You will need your passport to enter Morocco.

CHIPIONA

This town, just north of Rota on the Atlantic coast, is only about 20 minutes away—far enough to be an authentic Spanish rural town. In the summer, it is a popular destination for Spanish tourists, so the population doubles and the nightlife becomes more vibrant. In winter, the town is quiet, with donkeys and chickens in the fields.

The Chipiona Office of Tourism Website is:
http://www.turismochipiona.es/EN/index.html

Visit the website for more information about guided tours, and details about locations, times, and fees for the city's attractions. The Tourist Office is located in the castle.

There is plenty to see in Chipiona. The lighthouse is the tallest in Spain. You can climb 322 stairs to the top if you contact the tourism office in advance and pay a small fee. There are also free guided tours of the fishing *corrales*, which were developed by the Romans, but still used for fishing today. From the Tourist Center at the castle, you can turn down the walking street to find bars, restaurants, shopping, and local color. Or, you can follow the beachfront *paseo* (boardwalk) towards the Church of the Virgen de Regla. This beautiful church was originally built as a fortress, but is now a Franciscan monastery. From there, continue along the *paseo* to find Chipiona's most popular beach, Playa de Regla. Numerous restaurants and beach bars, such as Trinity Irish Bar or Picoco, offer lovely views.

Chipiona is famous for its Moscatel wine. Learn more at the Moscatel Museum (www.museodelmoscatel.com) or get a taste at several bodegas throughout the city. The Moscatel Wine Festival is celebrated every year in August. Other famous festivals in the city include the Carnaval in spring. This is not as big as the celebration in Cádiz, but much more family-friendly. The festival of El Pinar is an outdoor religious/tailgating adventure in early summer. Chipiona celebrates its patron saint, La Virgen de Regla, in September.

In between Chipiona and Rota is a newly developed resort area, Costa Ballena. It has its own beach, a golf course, parks with bike trails, and several playgrounds. It is a good location for surf schools, fishing tours, kite surfing lessons, or horse riding.

EL PORTAL (CARTHUSIAN HORSES)

Andalusian horses are a unique, beautiful breed that is important to Spanish history and culture. There are several options to see them. You can take lessons or go for a ride at one of the ranches near base. You can witness the training that has made them world-famous at the 'dancing horses' show in Jerez (details on page 165.) Or, you can visit the stud farm in El Portal. This is the farm where the horses are bred, and the ranch literally controls the entire breeding line of Andalusian horses. The horses are not trained here, for the most part, only bred. They are open regularly for tours of the grounds, but every Saturday at 11 am they do a special tour and show for the public.

The ranch is called Yeguada de la Cartuja (Ranch of the Cartujano horses). The horses are named after the nearby Carthusian monastery, which handled their breeding and protected the bloodline for hundreds of years, until the ranch was somewhat recently transferred to the direction of a non-Carthusian, Hierro del Bocado. You can see the monastery from the ranch grounds. It can be visited and has a lovely gift shop, but is no longer involved with the horses.

The Saturday tours begin at 11 am, and will take you around the stable and show area. Tours are available in English, Spanish, French German, or Italian. You should make reservations in advance, and arrive prior to 11 am to pick up your tickets. A family package is available throughout the summer. Tickets are usually 10 Euros per person, but the family package lets you pay for 2 adults and 1 child, with all additional children free. During the tour, you can pet almost 100 horses poking their heads over their stall doors, and you can see the breeding mares in their field. You will also get to see the veterinary clinic for the horses. You can visit the carriage house, which has a great collection of a dozen different coaches of various sizes and styles. The Carthusian horses, with their long slender bodies, are not designed to be cart-horses. So they cannot pull a heavy coach. They are more often used for racing coaches, or for elegant events like bridal carriages, and taking tourists around the cities in Southern Spain.

The walking tour lasts less than an hour. As you tour the grounds, there will be horses walking, pulling carriages, and displaying their skills in the outdoor dirt area near the stables. Don't be too concerned about photo ops at that time, because you will have plenty of opportunities to see the exact same horses in the indoor arena for the show. Kids can ride the coaches for free after the indoor show. On Saturdays, the show is included in your tour price. The indoor arena has seating all around. There is no need to pay for the "special seating" because there are only about four rows of seating around the arena, and they all have great views of each event. The arena seating is on bleachers, which will be covered in dust from the performance, so dress accordingly. You may want to pack a lunch, since the show begins around Noon, lasts one hour, and only snacks, sodas, and beer are available for purchase at the arena.

The show begins with the heart-pounding experience of mares entering the ring to the sounds of flamenco music. These breeding mares are the spoiled divas of the farm. They are gorgeous creatures: sleek, low to the ground, and very long. They are well-fed and well-disciplined. Without any reins or bridles, they respond to the sound of a cracking whip—running rapidly in a circle in one direction, then on cue wheeling and reversing direction simultaneously. The show is broken into segments, each several minutes long. Each horse demonstration is followed by a carriage demonstration. So you will get to see about 10 different techniques of horse stepping, and 10 different types of carriages. Explanations of each event are given in Spanish and English, accompanied by vibrant music.

Although the farm focuses on breeding, not training, they include some well-trained horses in the show. The Carthusian horses are more closely related to Mustangs than to the racing Thoroughbreds we see in the Kentucky Derby, so their movements and actions are light and graceful. You will see a traditional exhibition of eight mares on a line, wearing bells, led by a caballero (cowboy) in traditional clothing. Other horses bounce, jump, and dance to the music or do a high-step on command.

El Portal is a small town located only about 25 minutes from base. Begin by heading toward Jerez, but at the traffic circle with the Bodega barrels, take the first exit towards El Portal. In 5 km, you will enter the town of El Portal. Just before the first traffic light, turn right at the sign for the Yeguada. Follow for another 5 km, and just as you go under an overpass bridge, the entrance to the ranch will be on your left, clearly marked as Yeguada de la Cartuja. Then follow the road back to the dirt parking lot. The farm is stroller-friendly. Even though it is built on a steep hill, there are ramps beside all the stairs.

EL PUERTO DE SANTA MARIA

For many Americans stationed here, Puerto—just 15 minutes from the Naval Base—is home. It is one of the most popular locations for off-base housing. There are a variety of neighborhoods close to the beach full of large houses, blossoming gardens, and swimming pools. It is also the location of numerous stores and restaurants, a small mall, a pleasant riverside walking area, the ferry to Cádiz, and the local train station. This city has plenty of culture to warrant multiple visits. The historical landmarks are the bullring, the Cathedral, and the Castle. Puerto has one of the oldest bull rings in this area, and one of the largest in Spain. It was completed in 1880 and took almost 100 years to complete. It hosts bullfights throughout the summer, and is used for other performances in the off-season.

El Puerto de Santa Maria Tourist Office website:
http://www.turismoelpuerto.com

The tourist offices are located near the castle, at Plaza de Castillo or at the Valdelagrana Beach, at Paseo Maritimo. Visit for info about local events, festivals, walking tours, etc.

The Cathedral was built in the 16th century, in the High Gothic style. The main portion of the church collapsed in the 17th century, and was rebuilt in the Baroque style. The main altar was constructed even later, in the Neo-Classic style. There are numerous chapels dedicated to our Lady, who is always attired like a Queen. They are doing a massive restoration project, so some of the chapels have been restored to their original bright glimmers of gold. Religious festivals often have processions that start or end at the Cathedral.

The Castillo San Marco is a gorgeous structure combining Moorish and Christian architecture. It was originally a mosque, but was transformed into a church for the Christian king in the 13th century after the Moors were conquered. The walls and battlements were completed by the 15th century. You can take a tour of the original mosque area, which has been restored in modern times. You can even climb stairs up the walls to walk the battlements and see towers with Latin inscriptions to Jesus. The castle is now used for wedding receptions and formal events, but public tours are available weekly for a small entrance fee.

The city has interesting historical interest to Americans. Christopher Columbus spent time in this area gathering his crew for the expedition to the 'New World.' He was a guest of wealthy families in Puerto, and some of the houses where he stayed still stand. When he first sailed across the Atlantic and discovered the Americas, he took three ships: the Niña, the Pinta, and the Santa Maria. The Santa Maria was the largest ship, and was named for the city of El Puerto de Santa Maria.

Puerto is also part of the sherry triangle, and hosts several wonderful bodegas. The most famous is Osbourne, whose symbol is the black bull silhouette. When you visit a bodega, you will see large barrels of sherry, stacked on each other in rows labeled with dates and varieties of grapes. You will learn about the sherry-making process, see the wine-maker dip a slender metal rod called a *venencia* into the barrels, and then pour it through the air into small sherry glasses. You should be able to sample sherries ranging from dry whites to rich reds to sweet creams. Visit this website for information about local tours and tastings, in English:
 http://www.vinoybrandydelpuerto.com.

The best parking for the downtown historical section is in the area around the bull ring:
(GPS coordinates: 36°35'46.3"N 6°13'58.4"W)
or near the riverfront at the ferry station:
(GPS coordinates: 36°35'43.3"N 6°13'32.0"W).

GIBRALTAR

This town, just 1.5 hours from base, is huddled around the base of the famous Rock of Gibraltar. The colony is on the Spanish coast, but is actually part of the British Empire, so they speak English and serve British food. Because Gibraltar does not belong to Spain, you cross an international border when you go from the Spanish town of La Linea (the line) to the British peninsula of Gibraltar. So make sure to bring your passport! And because England is not part of the EU, this border crossing can be more complicated than going from Spain into Portugal or France. At the moment, there is political tension between Spain and Gibraltar, so Spain is threatening to impose tariffs on everyone crossing into Spain, and there are long lines of traffic to drive across the border. Currently, the easiest option is to pull into the large public paid parking lot right before the border, (GPS Coordinates: 36°09'19.0"N 5°21'15.2"W), pay a few Euros to park for the day, and walk across the border into Gibraltar. You need to show your passport and go through customs, but there are virtually no lines for foot traffic, and you pass through in just a moment, without even stopping to complete paperwork. You will then walk across the actual runway of Gibraltar's airport. It was tactically necessary to have an airstrip during World War II, but the peninsula is so small they had to build the runway extending into the bay.

Gibraltar has been a strategic location for its entire existence, and it is amazing how much of the town's history is influenced by warfare. Originally part of Spain because of geography, Gibraltar was ceded to the British by the Treaty of Utrecht "in perpetuity" in 1713. In exchange, Spain gained the territory of Florida (United States) from the British. Of course, Spain assumed that they could take back the city of Gibraltar at any time, and in 1726 they attempted to do so by a land blockade, but this was anticipated and repelled by the British. The Spanish tried again to reclaim Gibraltar during the Great Siege from 1779-1783. This time, they blockaded the town from the land and surrounded it with the Spanish Navy. But Gibraltar dug the famous siege tunnels into the Rock, and placed cannons there to repel the Spanish fleet. The sheer Rock was difficult to attack, and a landing was almost impossible. After a British sally at night against the Spanish fleet, the Spanish were again defeated. During World War II, Gibraltar once again became a contested territory. Franco, the dictator of Spain, was officially neutral, but supported Hitler during World War II. Gibraltar, as a British territory, was one of the few Allied toeholds into "fortress Europe." Hitler was eager to attack Gibraltar from Spain, and paid Franco a large bribe to allow his Nazi troops to move through Spain against Gibraltar. Franco accepted the bribe money, but then refused to allow the troops entrance, protecting Gibraltar from almost certain Nazi domination. During this time, the Allied troops rallied to defend Gibraltar, and built the airstrip across the narrow flat part of Gibraltar's peninsula. Numerous British naval vessels docked in Gibraltar's harbor, waiting for a Nazi attack. The airstrip and harbor are still of international importance today. The city is a major refueling point for ships of all nations heading into the Mediterranean.

After walking across the airport, visitors follow the main road into Gibraltar's town center, Casemates Square. It is about a 1 mile walk from the parking to the Square, but totally worth it to avoid traffic lines lasting 1-3 hours. There are currently no fees for pedestrians or cars to cross the border. Along the way, you will pass through the Landsport Tunnel, which was originally the only way to enter Gibraltar by land. Once in Casemates Square, you step into a quaint British town. The square is surrounded by pubs serving fish and chips, bangers and mash, pot pies, or delicious curry dishes. Waiters speak crisp British English, and you pay either in Euros or Gibraltar Pounds (different from British pounds). Gibraltar is a long, skinny town, with only one Main Street stretching over a mile along the base of the Rock. It was beautifully restored in 2000 to colonial British glory, so the atmosphere is very quaint, but the stores are quite modern, and there is an excellent selection of British clothing, food, and electronic stores for those who want to do some shopping.

There are two ways to reach the top of the Rock: by cable car, or by van taxi tour. The van taxis are currently a much better option. Numerous private companies display their ads or approach you on the street. They charge the same rates as you would pay to ride the cable car: 7 Euros to get to the top, and 7 Euros for entrance fees to the sights of St. Michael's Cave and the Great Siege Tunnels, for a total of 14 Euros per person. (Some companies charge 28 Euros per person.) Kids are free in the taxi van option, but would have to pay for the cable car. Also, the taxis make for a LOT less walking. The top of the Rock is longer than the town of Gibraltar itself, and there is additional walking to go through the Cave and Tunnels. So it would take most of the day to ride the cable car, walk several miles around the top, and see everything. With a taxi you can do that whole trip and see everything at a leisurely pace in just over 1 hour. The taxi first takes you to the Pillars of Hercules, at the southern tip of the Rock. This is Spain's southernmost point, and you can see Africa across the sea. In ancient history, Gibraltar was considered one of the Pillars of Hercules, with the other one being in Tangier, Morocco. Beyond these pillars, the ancients were not sure that there were any additional lands or civilizations. The pillars are still featured on Spain's coat of arms and national flag. The second location on the tour is St. Michael's cave. This is a natural limestone cave in the Rock. Over time, huge stalactites and stalagmites have formed. During the Great Siege, the cave was used as a bomb-proof hospital. Now, it is used for classical concerts. There are colorful light displays, and secure walkways and ramp areas for tourists.

The Rock's most famous residents are the Barbary apes. These wild monkeys have lived on the Rock for centuries, supposedly brought over on ships from Africa. The locals are very fond and proud of them. They are quite familiar with tourists, and will eagerly eat any snacks or candy. They will also climb all over you and harass you, so some people are terrified of them. This is when it is useful to have a taxi tour guide who knows each one! The central home of the apes is the Apes Den, at the crown of the Rock, but they can be found in areas all over the Rock.

The final stop on the taxi tour, and one of the most important attractions, is the Great Siege tunnels. These were carved by hand into the Rock during the Great Siege of 1779-1783. The tunnels allowed cannons to be brought up into the Rock, to fire upon the Spanish Armada below. Several cannons are still present in the tunnels, and visitors can peek out the windows into the harbor. There are also historical displays and wax figures throughout the tunnels, showing how they were constructed and explaining the politics and military strategy used during the Siege. The tunnels stretch over a mile inside the Rock. The walk is very interesting and informative.

To dip your toes in the Mediterranean, you have to get a car or taxi ride to the far side of the peninsula of Gibraltar. The beach on the Mediterranean side is very narrow, with only a single road running on that side of the peninsula.

JEREZ

Jerez (pronounced Hair-eth) is a beautiful and important city, about 30 minutes from Rota. For some Americans, it is known for the Luz Shopping Center, which contains an Ikea, Decathalon, Bricor, many other stores, and restaurants. (More info about shopping can be found in Part II of this book.) It also contains the closest civilian airport, with frequent connections to Madrid. But internationally, Jerez is famous for two things: sherry and horses. Jerez is the most well-known city in the sherry triangle. In fact, the word 'jerez' is the Spanish word for sherry, and the city received the name in Roman times, when the production of sherry began. The fortified wine has been an important product and export since that time. Now, Jerez is home to one of the world's most well-known sherry bodegas: Gonzalez Byass, home of Tio Peppe. This is a huge bodega in a beautiful setting. You can take tours in English with groups of tourists, and learn about the sherry-making process, sample the full range of sherry flavors, and even watch mice drink sherry. Visit http://www.bodegastiopepe.com/en/ to make a reservation.

The Jerez tourism website is:
http://www.turismojerez2.com

The tourist office is located at Plaza del Arenal.

The Andalusian horses can be seen at two different locations: the stud farm in El Portal (discussed on page 158) or the Andalusian Horse School in Jerez: Real Escuela Andaluza del Arte Equestre. The Real Escuela is an amazing display of the grace and elegance of these world-famous horses. They are bred for beauty, and are highly trained to obey verbal or touch commands, even without reins. The show is about 90 minutes long, and held in a beautiful indoor arena surrounded by rows of seating on all sides. The performance is called "How the Andalusian Horses Dance." It features the skills of traditional herding, classical dressage, carriage driving, and work in hand (when the trainer stands on the ground)—all accompanied by classical Spanish music. You will see horses stand on their hind legs, walk backwards, march in time to the music, and even perform a military step where they fully extend each front leg before stepping forward. One of our favorites was seeing a horse begin to run across the arena, then come to an instant stop. The show concludes with a carefully choreographed "dance" performed simultaneously by a large group of horses and riders. You will see horses weave among each other, and walk with their heads carefully held downward to the side. Tickets are rather expensive (17 Euros for children, 27 Euros for adults in 2014), but definitely worthwhile for any horse-lover to experience such a rare and artistic element of Spanish culture. Shows are usually on Tuesdays and Thursdays at Noon, with occasional Saturday performances. Visit their website at http://www.realescuela.org/en/ to learn more. It is also worth noting that you can also see gorgeous horse and carriage demonstrations during the Jerez Feria, held every spring.

Several other sites in Jerez are worth a visit. The Alcázar, or castle, was a Moorish fortress. You can still tour its mosque, Arab baths, and gardens. The main Cathedral is a 14th century construction built in the baroque style. Jerez has a small Archaeology Museum, with locally-discovered pieces ranging from Roman times through the 11th century when the Moors built up the city. The collection is predominantly pottery and small statuary, but the 300-year history of settlement and conquest in this region is fascinating. Jerez also has a zoo, a bee farm, a laser tag center and a go-kart track, all discussed in the Field Trips section earlier in this chapter, on pages 142-145.

For entertainment, Jerez is a great location to see flamenco shows. ITT hosts monthly trips to tour a bodega and see a flamenco show in Jerez, but there are numerous other locations to choose from. During a show, you can hear traditional Spanish guitar music and see dancers in thick shoes and ruffled dresses stomp, clap, and whirl to the music. Flamenco dance and music are rich and passionate, rooted in the gypsy culture that was formerly so strong in Andalusia. In the first week of May, Jerez is the host of the World Motorcycle Championship Grand Prix at the Circuito de Jerez, so be prepared for extra crowds and traffic that weekend.

Finally, I should mention that every June and July, the fields around Jerez are full of blooming sunflowers. This beautiful crop is a staple in this region, and is harvested for the seeds. It is perfectly legal to stop by a field and take pictures, but be sure to get permission from the farmer before entering a field or touching his crop.

MEDINA SIDONIA

Medina Sidonia is a lovely village perched on a mountain about 45 minutes from Rota. The name of the city is actually Arabic. It means 'city of Sidon.' This is perhaps a reference to the Phonecians, who originally settled here. Medina Sidonia has a lot to offer: Roman ruins, a history museum, gorgeous views, and some pretty good pastries. Park in the parking area of Plaza La Zapata (GPS Coordinates 36°27'29.9"N 5°55'36.1"W) and walk up several steep areas, along Calle Maripérez, Calle Manso, and Calle Arrieros to reach the main church. The views are worth it! Start your tour at the plaza in front of the town's main church: Santa Maria la Mayor. Like many other Spanish churches, it is a Renaissance style church that was built on the site of a mosque. Now, only the lower portion of the bell tower contains any remnants of the mosque. If you climb up the steps from the Plaza near the church, you will reach the ruins of a castle that was built in the 13th century. It is clear to see why a strong defensive position was necessary here: Medina Sidonia commands sweeping views of the valleys all around it. The Romans, the Moors, and the Spanish all used this city as a stronghold. Each civilization built on top of its predecessors, and the castle is at the top of the heap. Unfortunately, it is mostly in ruins now.

The city's museum, Museo Municipal, is located on Calle de Ortega. It is a small, yet very interesting building that demonstrates what life was life in the 1800's in Medina Sidonia. The first room displays agricultural equipment and tools. Other rooms show the contrast between the upper and lower classes in the 1800's. You can see dining rooms and sleeping quarters decorated in period artifacts from Medina Sidonia's wealthiest citizens. Those who were not upper class did not enjoy the same lavish lifestyle. They dined at smaller tables, and sat on chairs woven from rushes. Without fireplaces, their source of warmth was a small brazier of coals located under the table to warm those who sat around it. They slept on straw mattresses, which were too dangerous to be heated by any coals. Medina Sidonia became an important ducal seat in 1440. When traveling inland from Cádiz, Medina Sidonia was the next important town.

You can go even further back in time into the Roman foundations of the city. Inside are well-preserved Roman roads and Roman sewer systems. As the rest of the city was built upon the

Roman buildings, these tunnels were left intact. Don't worry, the sewers are dry and have no smell at all! The architecture of anything Roman is always impressive in its details and precision.

Medina Sidonia is the pastry capital of the Cádiz province. The local specialty is a shortbread roll called *alfajor* with almond and fig flavors. It is very rich and flavorful. The best version can be found at the Church of Santa Maria de la Victoria in their attached bakery. The nuns also make assorted flavors of cookies. A package of 6 large cookies is 3 Euros.

Just past the Iglesia de la Victoria is the main Plaza de España, and the town hall. The Plaza has several good restaurants surrounding it, as well as a bakery established in the 1800's. This is another good source of pastries if you are planning to bring some home. Just east of this Plaza is the main parking lot, with GPS coordinates listed on the preceding page. You can spend a pleasant day in Medina Sidonia, soaking in thousands of years of history, enjoying gorgeous mountaintop vistas, experiencing a quaint *pueblo blanco*, and tasting local delicacies. Enjoy this jewel of a village less than an hour from Rota!

RONDA

Ronda is a unique town, a favorite with tourists and visitors. The 'old town' was originally built on the mountain, possibly in Roman times, and the whole city was surrounded by a deep river gorge. Then it was conquered by the Moors in the 800's, and remained under their influence for several centuries. In the 1400's, they decided to expand beyond the gorge, building several bridges across it, and a sprawling city on the other side. The most famous landmark is the Puente Nuevo, the 'new bridge,' which is actually over 200 years old. The city has Arab baths (13th century) and some Roman ruins outside. The edges of Ronda end abruptly either at the gorge, or on the side of the mountain, so the city has gorgeous views of the surrounding hillsides.

The bullring is Ronda's other famous landmark. Bullfighting was supposedly invented in Ronda, and they have the oldest bullring in Spain. Apparently bullfighting developed when nobles used to train on horseback chasing bulls. One day, a nobleman fell off, and a servant quickly waved his colorful hat to distract the bull and keep the man from danger. Everyone thought it was a great sport, and the man soon added a retinue of mounted and un-mounted assistants to help with his fights. They are today's *picadores (*mounted*)* and *matadores* (un-mounted). Some of the most famous bullfighters fought here, and their statues can be seen around the city. The American author Ernest Hemingway spent time in Ronda, and the city's Spanish flavor and style is evident in his writing.

On summer mornings, Ronda is a huge favorite with tour groups, and has a crowded touristy feel. If you go in the afternoon or colder season, you will have the city to yourself. The Puente Nuevo is in the center of town. You can still drive or walk over it, but you have to go through the town to the sides of the cliff to actually see what the bridge looks like. Most busses park in the newer side of town, and then groups walk across the Puente Nuevo to reach the Old Town, with its narrow streets and winding medieval layout. If you can find space, you can drive through Old Town to a small parking lot at the end (GPS Coordinates: 36°44'10.4"N 5°09'55.0"W). From there, walk through a small park, past the church, and past several tourist shops. Begin your cliffside walk on Calle Real, in the Northeast area of the old town, at the stone arch of Felipe V. The arch was built during the Renaissance, and leads to a series of bridges, terraces, and steps that take you to the other side of the city. There are several options to get a view of the bridge. Near this arch is the entrance to Ronda's other famous attractions: the Arab Baths, Gardens, and Mines near the bottom of the cliff. You must pay a few Euros to enter the path to those sites, entered through the Terrace marked "Palacio del Rey Moro" near the stone archway. The path descends to the bottom of the gorge, and includes ancient stone steps cut into the cliff side. A more stroller friendly choice is the mild walk down paved terraces on the east side of the city. The public cliffside terrace walk is free. Along the way, you will have dizzying views of the gorge beside you, and then directly under you.

When you finally get a view of the bridge, it is amazing! It was constructed from the bottom of the gorge upward, so there are 3 different levels of arches. Even the lowest arch is still high over the river: we saw birds flying through that arch, while we looked down from a lofty terrace. Shortly before the path heads back towards the city, there is a great terrace for a photo op of your group with the bridge in the background. The terrace path ends on the newer side of the river. Here you can follow Calle Rosario back to the bridge, or to the famous Bullring. From the bullring, you can also take a carriage ride through the city.

Ronda's bullring was constructed in the 1700's, and was home to one of Spain's most famous bullfighters: Pedro Romero. It is a gorgeous structure that is almost a temple to the sport of bullfighting. Inside, you can tour the ring, and visit the Bullfighting Museum and the Royal Saddlery. Tickets are about 7 Euros per person (2014) and can be purchased on site, or by visiting:
http://www.rmcr.org/es/english.html.

Near the bullring, the Alamadeda del Tajo park has beautiful shaded boulevards, classic statues, and gorgeous views of the sun setting over the mountains. It is a great spot to enjoy a break, or let the kids run and play. Finally, Ronda's Parador Hotel sits at the Northern end of the bridge, and the outdoor terrace has amazing views of the bridge and gorge. This is a great place to enjoy a coffee or snack. Your family and visitors will certainly appreciate the dramatic landscape and rich Spanish culture in Ronda!

ROTA

Rota is just outside the base's main gate, and is usually the first place visitors explore. The town is old, with narrow streets, whitewashed buildings, and a cathedral and castle from the 15th century. But it also has a modern vibe, because of the intense renovations that have occurred around the beaches and harbor area. The beachside *paseo* (boardwalk) is broad and flat, and stretches along the beaches on both sides of the city. During the summer, you can stroll the *paseo*, enjoy some *helado* (ice cream), and stop at a *chiringuito* (beach bar) for a cool sangria or mojito. Tourists flood the city in summer, nearly doubling the population, and providing vibrant nightlife in clubs. In winter the town is quiet, but you can still enjoy the waves, the fresh seafood, and the small shops and bakeries.

One way to tour Rota is by visiting the Welcome to Rota center, just outside the base gate. They offer free tours weekly, using the little tourist train to drive around town and visit sites of interest. They always stop at a restaurant to enjoy free tapas during the tour, but locations change weekly. The Center staff are very friendly and able to answer any questions about the city, where to find things, etc.

To visit the town on your own, you can park on base and walk through the main gate into town. From there, walk downhill toward the lighthouse and the harbor area. One of Rota's main beaches, Playa del Rompidillo, will be on your left. At the harbor, you can stop by the fish market—the small low building on you left when facing the lighthouse—to purchase fresh-caught seafood. Or walk out on the point to watch the waves crash against the rocks. Round the point, and walk along the paseo a short distance until you come to the pointed archway pictured on this book's cover. The stones are coral, mined from the reef just offshore. The original builders used coral blocks to build the castle, cathedral, and city walls. If you look closely, you can see little shells in the stone. Through the archway, you will see the Cathedral straight ahead of you. Walk towards it, and you will arrive at Plaza Bartolomé Pèrez, the main square between the Cathedral and the castle. It is named for a man from Rota, who sailed with Columbus to discover the Americas. The Castle, *Castillo de la Luna*, contains the tourism office and is free to enter. It was obviously built with Moorish influence. In fact, the Spanish invited the Moors into this region in the 8th century to help fight the Goths coming down from France. The Moors stayed until the 15th century when they were finally forced out. Most castles in this area were built by the Moors, since the south was their last stronghold. Every Moorish palace and mosque has a fountain or pool in the center, because ritual washing is an important part of Moorish (Muslim) traditions, and a well guaranteed fresh water during a siege. The fountain in this castle is made with traditional "Spanish" tile, *azuletes* which was brought from Africa by the Moors. There are beautiful examples of Moorish artwork everywhere, but on one side of the castle courtyard you can see the original painted tiles. They are 1000 years old! The castle is now used as City Hall, and the former chapel is now the main courtroom. Rota's emblem is a castle surrounded by the rosary, because Our Lady of the Rosary is the city's patron saint.

**Rota's Visitor Center is located in the Castle.
Their website is:
http://www.aytorota.es**

**You can also visit the Welcome to Rota Center located
just outside the Rota Gate.**

Across the plaza is the town cathedral, the center of most religious feasts and holidays. Many Spanish cathedrals are in the Renaissance Baroque style of the 1500's. That's the case of this cathedral's side chapel, although the rest of the church is a little older and less ornate. The main rule of Baroque style is to leave no blank space. So the artists and builders filled the chapel with gilded carvings, paintings, and scrollwork. The rest of the church is much darker. There were windows behind the main altar, but the glass broke during the Lisbon earthquake hundreds of years ago, so they have been sealed with stone.

At this point, you can continue walking along the paseo and eat at a restaurant overlooking the ocean. Or, you can wander the narrow streets behind the castle, exploring small restaurants offering everything from pizza to kebabs to traditional Spanish tapas. Follow Calle Higuereta for the most food options. To return to base, walk uphill along Av. San Fernando, past the traffic circle with the giant hands. Just past the circle with the Mary fountain, you will see Base.

SANLÚCAR HORSE RACES

Every August, in the nearby town of Sanlúcar de Barrameda, there is a series of horse races on the beach! The races, called *carreras de caballos de Sanlúcar*, have been held at this location since about 1845, so they are one of the oldest horse races in Spain. Races are held on two separate weekends, usually the 1st and 3rd weekend of August. They are scheduled around the low tide on the Guadalquivir river, around 6:30 pm, and last until sunset, around 10 pm. Each race is about 1 mile, so they only last a few moments, but there is a new race every 45 minutes. This is a great event for the whole family. Sanlúcar is 40 minutes from base. Enjoy a day at the beach, a beautiful sunset, and some thrilling horse races!

To attend the races, you do not need tickets. Spaces on the beach are available on a first-come basis. If you go before 5 pm, the Spanish will still be at siesta, so there will be plenty of room. On the other hand, if you are going with children and don't want to wait around for hours, you will still be able to squeeze in anywhere after 7 pm. There are stands set up near the finish line, and for 10 Euros per person you can have an unobstructed view, plus enjoy some food and entertainment from the cassettas. Anywhere else on the beach is free. Bring some beach toys and snacks, or buy drinks and snacks from the vendors pushing wheelbarrows along the beach.

Parking is available at Sanlúcar's main underground parking lot: GPS Coordinates (36°46'56.9"N 6°21'24.0"W). Follow the feria grounds two blocks to the riverfront, and you will be near the starting line. Or, when the reach the river, turn left and walk up to one mile, and you will reach the finish line. Once at the beach, you will see numerous home-made cardboard stands. These are betting booths, run by the Spanish children. The bets are small, usually just pocket change, but the kids take it very seriously. They issue tickets and pay out dividends after each race. They are probably the youngest bookies you'll ever see.

In between races, people can walk anywhere on the beach or play in the water. Before each race, the police will clear the beach and move everyone behind a fence. A tractor moves the starting gate in between races, probably because of the changing low tide line. Then you'll see the jockeys walking their horses slowly down the beach toward the starting line. Some races only have four horses, others have up to eight, but each race is a small batch. The prize money is very prestigious—up to several thousand Euros—so these are very qualified riders and horses.

There was no starting bell or gunshot that we could hear, just a huge cheer from the crowd, and then they were off! You will hear a police siren, as a car races by ahead of the horses to clear the way. Everyone rushes to the fence, because the horses are just seconds behind. There is a plastic netting fence set up, and the crowd presses in at least four or five people deep. If you want a good view, you have to be right on the fence. The horses go by in a pounding blur!

After each race, the netting comes down, and everyone can play in the sand and the water. You will see fathers standing in the water, playing with their kids, with an alcoholic drink in one hand. The Spanish children are allowed to climb all over the starting gate. The atmosphere is relaxed, fun, and exciting. We were struck by how very Spanish this event is: children out late (past sunset), families talking and drinking together, and everyone just sharing the beach and enjoying an event together. If you are just there for the horse races, you may be a little bored, because they are 45 minutes apart, and only about three races each night. But if you are there to enjoy a family evening on the beach, with the added thrill of horses running by, you will have a blast!

SEVILLA

The gorgeous city of Sevilla is about 90 minutes North ot nase. There are so many reasons to visit Sevilla, and so much to explore, so I hope you will visit it several different times, in different seasons, to truly appreciate it. Sevilla is the largest city in this region, and is the capital of Andalusia. There are numerous chain restaurants and stores for those interested in American food or brand-name shopping. Culturally, the highlights are the Cathedral, the Alcázar, and the Plaza d'España. The Cathedral and Alcázar are located right across from each other. The Plaza d'España is several blocks south, just barely comfortable walking distance. You can take a carriage ride between the two locations, for a high price, or simply park between the two and walk. Driving tips: The drive along the major highway has one toll of 7.50 Euros in each direction (which you can bypass if you wish, but it is hardly worth the extra time). Parking is very difficult mid-day during peak tourist season. On weekends, if you arrive early, you can sometimes park directly behind the Plaza d'España on the streets that are marked for the University. Parking is available for up to 24 hours, and costs .20 Euro cents per hour. There is also public underground parking on Avenida Roma closer to the Cathedral. (GPS Coordinates: 37°22'52.8"N 5°59'36.9"W).

ALCÁZAR: One of the most stunning buildings in Sevilla, and possibly in Spain, is the Real Alcázar, or royal palace. (Real is actually pronounced 'Ray-al' and it means Royal, in Spanish.) The upper level is still used by the Royal Family when they are in town, so it is one of the oldest castles still in use in Europe. It is one of the best surviving examples of *Mudejar* architecture, which is the elaborate Moorish style of carvings in tile and stucco. The Courtyard of the Maidens (*El Patio de las Doncellas*), with its graceful Moorish arches, and detailed stucco work, is truly beautiful. The throne room glitters, and was designed to impress visitors and ambassadors from around the world. Every single door and window in the palace is a unique work of art. The palace was originally the site of a Moorish fort, but in 1364 the Christian King Pedro I ordered the construction of the royal residence that is there today. The finest craftsmen of Toledo and Grenada were enlisted to make a palace that amazes and glitters at every turn. The tiles show Islamic inscriptions, as well as the castle and lion figures that represent Queen Isabella and King Ferdinand. Unless you have visited the Alhambra in Granada, you will be unprepared for the breathtaking intricate artwork. Fans of the TV show *Game of Thrones* may recognize the palace as the location of the Dornish king's water garden palace in Season 5. It was filmed on location in 2014.

Several important marriages and births occurred here. It also became the central point through which all trade with the New World was conducted, and Isabella met with Columbus in the chapel here. The ceilings throughout the palace were designed to recognize some of these momentous events, and each one is unique. You are continually looking up at bright geometric designs, carved wood inlaid with gold, and gorgeous symbols. The most impressive ceiling is the one in the throne room. The dome directly over the king's throne is carved wood inlaid with pure gold. The stars represent the heavens, demonstrating that no one but God is higher than the king. The throne room and adjacent Hall of Ambassadors were made to impress visitors to the court of Spain. The Peacock Doorway is what ambassadors would pass through to enter the throne room. The triple horseshoe arches are used throughout the palace, and are typical Islamic style. Every surface is covered in gold or *azuletes* (blue tiles). A Christian palace built by Islamic artisans is interesting and truly amazing.

After the splendor of the palace, the gardens are a refreshing respite. Most of the palace is open-air and the complex is interwoven with several cooling courtyards. But the actual gardens are behind the Alcázar, and contain pleasant paths going to fountains, pools, and outlaying structures. They are well-maintained, and have some poetic verses and statuary scattered throughout. The pond you see upon entering the gardens was originally a Cistern, used to collect rainwater from the roofs. The rain spout still works, but it has now been modified into a still pond stocked with fish. The Spanish gardens are very structured, geometric, and beautiful. It is easy to picture the women of the Court in the 1400's spending their mornings or evenings there, enjoying the splash of the fountain and the cool breezes. Entrance fee to Alcázar and gardens: 8.50 Euros per adult. Summer Hours: 9:30 am- 7 pm Tuesday-Saturday, closes at 5 pm on Sundays. Winter Hours (Oct-March): 9:30 am- 5 pm Tuesday-Saturday, closes at 1:30 pm Sunday.

CATHEDRAL: Sevilla's Cathedral, like many in Spain, is built on the site of a former mosque. Most of the mosque was destroyed in an earthquake before the Christian site was constructed, although the Orange Courtyard remains essentially the same. You can still recognize the Moorish architecture in the domes of the building and the arches and windows. The famous Giralda bell tower is the former minaret of the mosque. The Giralda was added onto and re-decorated in several stages, but it is clearly the minaret that used to call Muslims to worship. Entry fee to the Cathedral, which includes access to the Giralda and Treasury: 8 Euros per person (2014).

The Cathedral was constructed between 1402 and 1506. During that time, Spain discovered the New World and enjoyed its Golden Age. Sevilla was the economic capital of Spain during the Golden Age, and all imports from the New World were sent directly upriver to this inland city. The Cathedral was intended to be a display of wealth and beauty that would be considered almost crazy. When it was completed, it replaced the Hagia Sophia in Turkey as the largest cathedral in the world. The nave (main aisle) is the longest in Spain, and the 3rd largest in the world. The ceilings are high, (42 meters) intricately carved and decorated. The building is fairly dark inside, due to very few stained glass windows. It also has a somewhat complicated design, since it is laid out in the shape of a cross, and gives the impression of being as wide as it is long. There are 80 chapels, all with their own theme and unique artwork. Inside, there are works of art, ornate carvings, and a chapel covered in gold.

Christopher Columbus is buried in the Cathedral. His tomb is carried by four figures wearing the lion heraldry of King Ferdinand and the castle symbol of Queen Isabella. Although he died in somewhat of a state of disgrace, having been rejected by the Caribbean islands as an inhumane governor, Christopher Columbus is still a hero in Spanish history because he discovered the Americas and brought enormous wealth to Spain.

If you climb the Giralda, you will have spectacular views of the city and the Cathedral itself. The inside of the bell tower is filled with a series of ramps (about 32 of them) which make for a somewhat breath-taking and crowded climb. You see different aspects of the Cathedral from each side of the Giralda. The main dome is off to the side of the Giralda. The dome collapsed soon after the church was constructed, and then again after the Lisbon Earthquake of 1888.

PLAZA D'ESPAÑA: Think, for a moment, about the year 1929. In America, the 'Roaring 20's,' Prohibition, and gangsters were all coming to an end, and we were about to plunge into the Great Depression. In Europe, the depressions that followed WWI (and led to WWII) were still raging in some countries, including Spain. Andalusia, in particular, suffered from poverty and joblessness. To assuage this economic situation and bring trade into the region, Spain organized the 1929 Ibero-American Exposition to be held in Sevilla. To host such an international event, they had to construct a park and permanent pavilions in the Parque Maria Luisa, which the Princess of that name had donated to the city in 1893. What remains is possibly the most gorgeous part of Sevilla: the Plaza d'España.

The Plaza is a long semi-circular building with tall towers at either end, enclosing a crescent-shaped pond with a plaza and a fountain in the center. The entire area is filled with tile work and hand-painted ceramics, so from handrails to lamp posts, everything here is a work of art. This is a wonderful place to take visitors and let them think, 'WOW, Spain is gorgeous!' And it's free and open to the public. Take some time to wander around the edges, studying the elaborate tile 'benches.' There are 50 huge tile benches, one for each province of Spain, including the Canary Islands. They are placed side by side around the entire semi-circle, in alphabetical order. Each province has a unique picture, hand-painted tile artwork, and a map showing where in Spain it is located. It is fun to look at them, but beware of gypsies hawking their wares all around!

The Plaza d'España is surrounded by the Parque Maria Luisa, which is a beautiful leafy area that is like a much classier version of Central Park. From the Plaza, you can take a carriage ride with one of the many horses that line up there, or you can just stroll the shaded gravel boulevards and enjoy the garden fountains, statues, and flowers. There are also large bicycles for rent that will seat a family of four on their wide bench seats.

If you wander to the Southeast of the Parque Maria Luisa, you will see some of the other pavilions that were constructed for the 1929 Exposition. They have been converted into museums, but the buildings themselves are quite interesting. Worthy of special mention is the Archaeology Museum. Admission is FREE to EU citizens (simply show your Spanish driver's license). The museum has several exhibits from Spain's pre-historic times and from the Phoenician civilization, but of course the 'cool stuff' is from the Roman period. There are numerous mosaics, statues, and ruins from the Roman site of Italica, just outside Sevilla, including larger-than-life statues and pillars from the Temple of Diana. The museum is three stories, with most exhibits on the two main floors. The English guide pamphlet has useful information about each room, but the rest of the descriptions are in Spanish, so bring a dictionary to get the most of your visit.

CERAMICS: Some people come to Sevilla just for the shopping! Triana is the ceramics district of Sevilla. If you cross the bridge from the bullring to the other side of the river, you will be in Triana. The prices and selection are good here, some of the best in Spain. There are numerous shops along the streets San Jacinto and Calle San Jorge. Parking is available in Plaza del Altazano. See samples from one shop at www.ceramicatriana.com. That gives you an idea of some of the colors and styles available here. You can sometimes find these ceramics at stores closer to base, or even in the NEX, but Triana offers the best variety and most competitive prices.

TANGIERS, MOROCCO

The African continent lies just across from Spain, with only a narrow portion of the Mediterranean Sea in between. It is possible to take a ferry from Tarifa, Spain to Tangiers, Morocco. It's a long day trip, but it will take you to a completely different world. Tangiers is exotic—filled with colorful tiles, doors, spices, rugs, new flavors, and smells. You can ride a camel, watch a snake charmer, taste mint tea, and enjoy some amazing food. However, Tangiers is also a 3rd world country with a somewhat dangerous melding of wealth and poverty. Classy hotels attract rich clients, while around the corner families beg and live in squalor. The vendors are relentless, almost desperate, in their pursuit of clients in the street. If you show any interest or make eye contact, you may find yourself in a frustrating negotiation that can last up to 15 minutes—even if you are walking away the entire time! Morocco is a foreign country with a foreign culture. Therefore, it is recommended that you visit Tangiers with a local guide, who can safely escort you to areas of interest, while protecting you from the intense pressure of street vendors. There are several trusted guides who have served the Rota community for years. Check with the Fleet and Family Center to get some recommendations, or ask friends who have recently traveled. A good guide will find out ahead of time where you want to go, meet you at the port with a car, provide transportation to areas of interest throughout the day, walk with you through the markets, assist with negotiations if you want to buy something, and allow you to keep purchases in the car during the day so you don't have to carry everything with you. Prices for a guide should be determined ahead of time, and are usually based on the size of the group and the length of the tour.

Note: Some people feel that Tangiers, as a port town, is too flooded with tourists and vendors to give an authentic Moroccan experience. If you are looking for a more genuine taste of Morocco, consider visiting the Moroccan blue town of Chefchaouen. It is further inland and less convenient to reach, but still possible as a day trip, with some of the same guides who work in Tangiers.

THINGS TO DO DURING A DAY IN MOROCCO:

- Ride a camel. There are many places to do this. Some charge one price for a photo and more for a ride. A guide can get you a fair deal and camels that don't look sickly.
- Visit the Kasbah. This is the former palace fort of the sultan. It is an impressive building with huge walls, and also now a historical museum. Entrance fees 10 dihrams.
- Tour the American Legation for Moroccan Studies. This is the only American museum on foreign soil, and has interesting history and art displays. Minimal entrance fee.
- Barter at the flea market. The *Casa Barata* flea market is an outdoor area with a wide range of spices, rugs, baskets, clay items, and even furniture for sale. The adjacent *souk* is an indoor market open twice a week.
- Watch a snake charmer. Depending on your interest in snakes, you can get VERY up close and personal with them!
- See the Cave of Hercules, a natural cave which has been expanded and modified since the time of the Phoenicians. Legends abound, stating that the cave has tunnels leading to Gibraltar, that Hercules built it, or that he simply slept there.
- Visit the Church of St. Andrew. It is an Anglican church built in 1894, and a unique blend of Moroccan and English architecture.
- Eat delicious food! Whether you enjoy kebobs, couscous, tagines, or mint tea, Tangiers has numerous high-quality restaurants and tea houses to enjoy.

Tips for the trip: Contact the Security office first, since Morocco is not always approved for American military personnel to visit. Bring your passport! You are in another country. Expect to change money. Morrocco uses the dirhram. Dress appropriately: even though you probably can't enter any mosques, remember that Morocco is a Muslim country. Women should wear pants or long skirts, and have their shoulders covered as well. Be prepared for a long day. Tarifa is 1 hour 15 minutes from Rota, and the ferry ride takes 45 minutes in each direction. And use common travelling sense—keep your belongings safe at all times, stay with a group, be aware of your surroundings, and don't buy anything you can't carry with you, even if they promise to ship to you later!

UBRIQUE

Did you know that some of the finest leather in Spain is artistically produced just 1.5 hours from Rota? Then you will be interested in visiting the town of Ubrique! The wonderful thing about Southern Spain is that there are so many little villages to discover. I knew that Ubrique specialized in producing leather products. What I didn't realize is that the town itself would be such an architectural gem in the middle of the Sierra de Grazelema mountains.

Parking: there is a large dirt lot at the lower Eastern end of the city, at the end of Doctor Zarco Bohorquez street. Parking is free, and you can easily walk to leather shops or anywhere else in the city. If you are looking for the leather shops, stay in the lower section of town, near the river. The Spanish word for leather is *piel*, and you will recognize the leather shops because of their attractive window displays. There are many good ones side by side on Doctor Solis Pascual and Avenida España.

The shops sell a variety of gorgeous leather products: purses, wallets, belts, jackets, gloves, and even accessories like cell phone cases and desk supply organizers. Everything is hand-made, sometimes with layers and colors of leather, and there are stamped and embossed products as well. Everything in Ubrique is a work of art. The process of tanning, cutting, and tooling the leather has been practiced there for over 100 years, with skills passed down from generation to generation. The leather products range from 20 Euro wallets to leather coats that are several hundred Euros. They are certainly gorgeous and unique gifts.

If you go during July or January, you can benefit from the national sales that give huge discounts on the entire inventory of every store. Be aware that the stores will all be closed during siesta, from 2-5 pm, so be prepared to get into town early and do your shopping before 2 pm. Ubrique is about 90 minutes from Rota.

When you finish shopping (or if you arrive during siesta), take some time to explore this quaint village. The city spreads out into the valley, and straddles the Rio Ubrique, the tiny river canal that runs through town. Ubrique is a beautiful *pueblo blanco*, a white-washed village built right up against a steep mountain cliff. You can wander the streets working your way up towards the church of San Antonio, with stunning red and white architecture, which is located near the highest point of the city. When you reach the top of the town, you will see that some houses are literally built into the mountainside, around rocks that jut out of the mountain cliff! The streets are rather steep, but the views make the climb completely worthwhile. You definitely get a classic Andalusian feel in this town: white-washed walls, steep narrow cobblestone streets, unexpected gardens and bright potted plants. There are plenty of restaurants in the lower area of the city near the leather shops, but there are also tiny bakeries to enjoy in the winding narrow streets. Ubrique is a gorgeous white village to explore, even if you are just window shopping. I would recommend the trip to anyone!

VEJER DE LA FRONTERA

Vejer de la Frontera is another ancient white village (*pueblo blanco*) perched on the top of a hill, about 1 hour South of Rota. It was a settlement during Phoenician and Roman times, then taken over by the Moors in the 8th century, and remained in their control until the reign of the Christian kings in the 13th century. Then Vejer became a frontier town for the war between the Christians and Moors, which is why it still has the title "de la Frontera." The city walls, several churches, the old castle, and the beautiful fountain in the Plaza de España all show examples of Moorish architecture. From the highest points you can enjoy beautiful views of the ocean and the surrounding valleys stretching for miles in all directions. You can even see Morocco on a clear day! Much of the ancient city walls and gates are still intact, so this is a wonderful city to just wander through and soak up the history and culture of this region. Be prepared for lots of narrow streets and uphill walking. A large parking lot is available at the lower end of the town off the N-340 road. (GPS Coordinates: 36°15'21.9"N 5°58'03.2"W.) The tourist information center is located next to this parking lot.

Vejer is also well known for its running of the bulls, which takes place every year on Easter Sunday. There is no bullfight, but there are usually two runnings. One bull at a time is released into the streets on this day. Barricades are set up to protect onlookers, but anyone running in the streets will have to climb windows or run for cover when the bull charges through! Military personnel are not permitted to run with the bull, but they may watch the event, which has its own unique festival atmosphere.

There are many great restaurant choices in Vejer, but the most popular and well-known is the Moroccan style restaurant beneath the hotel off the Plaza de España, called El Jardin del Califa. The building itself is a historic monument dating from the 1500's, and the stone courtyard is an exotic location to relax and enjoy a great meal. The restaurant serves amazing selections of Moroccan dishes like tagine, kabobs, falafel, cous cous, barbequed meat, and salads. Advance reservations are recommended, as this restaurant is very popular! It has been listed in the Michelin guide for the past few years.

Finally, there are several important landmarks to note nearby. The Roman city of Baelo Claudia (described on pages 151-152) is in the nearby town of Bolonia, and both cities can easily be visited in the same day. In addition, the famous naval Battle of Trafalgar was fought in the waters just off the coast of Vejer. During this battle in 1805, the British Admiral Lord Nelson achieved a crushing victory over the combined Spanish-French fleet, and did not lose a single ship from the British Navy. This is not a fond memory for the Spanish, since it marks the end of Spanish maritime superiority. However, there is a tall monument commemorating the battle on the top of Cape Trafalgar.

ZAHARA DE LA SIERRA

ïouthern Spain, November marks the beginning of the olive harvest season. Fresh olive oil is pressed from November through January in a process known as a cold press. You can witness the process in the village of Zahara de la Frontera, one of the *pueblos blancos*, or white villages, that dot the mountainsides in this region. Just over 1 hour of driving brings you into some gorgeous mountains. They are rocky and rugged, with steep cliffs and distinctive outlines. Everywhere, neat rows of olive trees cover the hills.

The town of Zaharra, with its distinctive castle on the mountain crest and the rest of the town sprawled out below, is a picturesque destination any time of year. The whole town is surrounded by a National Park and overlooks a man-made reservoir famous for water sports. It is also a great destination for hiking, as described on page 146). If the ground is too wet for harvesting machinery, you could see workers on the hills gathering olives the old-fashioned way: spreading blankets beneath the trees, then beating the trees with sticks until all the ripe fruit falls.

An olive mill called El Vinculo is just outside Zahara. It has been in operation since 1755. The process today is still mostly the same as it was then, except now they have machines to do work that was previously done by animals. It is a fairly small place: The oil extracting is done in the mill, *La molina*, on the left side of the courtyard, and the products are sampled and sold in the store on the right side of the courtyard. In the courtyard itself are the former presses, used before hydraulics were invented.

The process of extracting olive oil, or 'olive juice', is very similar to the process of extracting cider from apples. First, the olives are poured into hoppers and shaken on elevated conveyor belts to separate the leaves from the fruit. The olives are washed, and then poured into a large vat which not only blends them into a pulp (with pits inside) but also allows them to be heated in a water bath that is just below boiling. The bath is heated with wood only, not natural gas, because the pulp would absorb those fumes. So they have to use wood from old olive trees. It has to be kept at a constant temperature so it won't break down the acids in the oil. Once the olives have been turned into a heated pulp, they are ready to be squeezed. Woven circular mats, with a hole in the center, are thrown over a metal pole. The pole rotates in a circle, while the olive pulp is pumped onto it. Then another mat is placed on top, and coated with another layer of olives. This continues until you have a full stack, about 8 feet high. At this point, the mats catch the solid materials, and the oil starts to ooze out. But to really extract the oil, you need to apply pressure with a hydraulic press. The entire mat/pulp stack is moved across the room by forklift to the row of pressing machines. Using hydraulic presses to achieve a very high PSI, all liquid is extracted from the olives and the mats. What's left is a dry mud-like substance, which is fed to pigs. The oil is either bottled right away, or stored in giant tanks.

The reason we call it "Extra Virgin" olive oil is because that oil comes from the first pressing. It has the purest, strongest flavor. Additional pressings are possible, but produce much lesser quality oil. The greatest enemy of olive oil is sunlight. Over time, sun breaks down the chemicals in the olive oil, making it turn more clear and tasteless. If stored at a constant temperature without sun exposure, the oil can last forever. Historians have actually unearthed oil jars from ancient shipwrecks, and the olive oil in them was still good because of the lack of sunlight or temperature change. But in our houses, since the bottle sits on the counter and gets indirect sun exposure, it is only good for about a year.

After watching the demonstration, stop by the on-site shop to enjoy some free samples. The oil is so rich and delicious that it has its own great flavor and smell. They sell a variety of qualities of oil in the shop, as well as wine, and products like olive soap and table olives.

You can then take a short, steep walk through town, to the square in front of the church. Along the way, take in the gorgeous panoramic view of the mountains. The restaurant at the square appears to be one of the only restaurants in town, but the food is delicious. There is also a pastry shop on the square. If you have the energy and enthusiasm, you can make the hike to the castle on top of the hill, which is in some disrepair, but still provides amazing views!

WEEKEND TRIPS

ome of these locations CAN be reached in a day, but if you wa.... to actually explore the town, a weekend is recommended. Of course, with a weekend you can fly to almost any destination in Europe, so only weekend *driving* trips are listed in this section.

Some locations in Spain can be reached in a weekend, such as Valencia in the East, Barcelona in the Northeast, or Compostela (pilgrimage church) in the North. However, you would still need to fly or take a fast train to these destinations, since they are around 12 hours driving by car.

If you are looking to spend a luxury weekend at an all-inclusive hotel or resort, popular destinations are Albufueria or Lagos along the Atlantic coast in Southern Portugal, or Estepona or Marbella in Spain, along the Mediterranean coast. Use any hotel search website to check out these locations and read reviews of resorts to find one that matches your taste. Remember that tiny towns near the big tourist centers will have the same great beaches and views, but with cheaper accommodations.

If you are up for a half-day drive, and spending a weekend doing historical or cultural exploring, then keep reading...

CÓRDOBA

Córdoba, (pronounced with the emphasis on the first syllable) in Southern Spain is the capital of the Córdoba province, and was formerly the Muslim capital of the caliphate, when the Moors were in control of central Spain. Córdoba is about 3.5 hours from base. The city is landlocked between two major mountain ranges. It is strategically located on the Guadalquivir River, which runs westward through Sevilla and to the Atlantic Ocean. During the peak of Moorish rule, Cordoba was a rival to Baghdad in wealth and culture. The Moors exported wine and oil from Spain. In the 10th century, in the middle of the 'Dark Ages,' Córdoba was one of the most populated cities of Europe, with a population of 1 million, a large library and a famous university. The jewels of this wealthy city were the Great Mosque, or *Mezquita*, and the Royal Palace, or *Alcázar*.

MEZQUITA: In 784, under the leadership of the caliph Abd-al Rahman, construction began on a great Mosque on the site of an old Visigoth church. The most striking feature is the red and white arches. In the original mosque, these are made of brick and stone in alternating bands, and are remnants of the Visigoth church. The moors stacked the arches in a double layer to achieve the desired height. The rows of columns and arches are said to imitate palm and date trees in a desert oasis. The original design was a building full of light, but later renovations (including the construction of a Christian cathedral in the center of the structure) have made it rather dim and hushed inside. Later caliphs expanded on the layout of the mosque in every direction. In the newer sections, instead of using brick and stone, they painted red and white bands onto the arches. The layout of the mosque and some of the decoration are said to imitate the Great Mosque of Damascus. The red and white stripes imitate the interior of the Dome of the Rock in Jerusalem. The Muslim caliphs had wealth and power to import the best artisans and the finest supplies for the construction of the mosque. This extravagance is most evident in the area called the Mihrab, which is the prayer 'niche' (more like a large area) in the Eastern wall that is aligned with Mecca. From the Mihrab, the imam would read from the Koran. The area is decorated with solid gold tiles, and designed so that the reader's voice will carry out into the mosque to his audience.

When the Christians re-conquered Cordoba in 1236, the mosque was designated as a Christian church. By the 14th century, construction began on a Renaissance cathedral that literally rises out of the center of the mosque. To build the cathedral, numerous columns and arches were destroyed, and those that remained were decorated with crosses and Christian bas-relief sculptures. The conversion of the building probably saved it from destruction during the Inquisition, when many other mosques were destroyed. The cathedral is rather beautiful, and full of light, but it is in definite contrast to the rest of the building. In fact, even though the Christian king Charles V gave permission for the cathedral's construction, he later commented upon seeing it, "you have taken something unique in all the world, and destroyed it to build something which could be found in any city."

Admission fee to the Mezquita is 8 Euros per person. It is FREE in the mornings from 8- 9:30 am. Morning Mass is celebrated daily at 9:30 am, so admittance is not permitted between 9:30 and 10 am, and then you can enter the mosque area, but must wait for Mass to finish before entering the Cathedral.

ALCÁZAR: This was the palace of King Ferdinand and Queen Isabella after the Catholic re-conquest of Córdoba. There was formerly a Visigoth fortress on the site, but construction on the palace began in 1328. Over the years, it was used as a fortress and a prison. Excavations are underway in some areas, but the castle has not been fully restored. The gardens are the real draw for visitors. One can spend at least an hour wandering among the organized flower beds and gorgeous fountains. The gardens of the Alcázar are a beautiful example of Moorish and Spanish design. The Moors built central fountains to cool their patios and gardens, and to provide the sound of splashing water. These gardens were more impressive than those at the Alcázar in Sevilla because of the elaborate irrigation planning. The major pools and fountains were laid out in a stepped pattern, each level slightly lower than the previous, so that water could flow downhill to each area. The garden has multiple pools, each surrounded by different colors of flowers, with each flower bed irrigated through tubes in the ground. Where does all the water come from? Before the Christian kings built the Alcázar, the Moors had developed irrigation using water wheels on the Guadalquivir River.

There is a replica of a large water wheel near the Roman bridge, which was used to pump water into the Alcázar gardens. The Moors developed the system of cisterns and trenches to move water throughout the garden. The result is a lush, cooling paradise in the middle of a rather hot, dry land.

Although the castle itself is not fully restored, it is possible to tour the chapel, towers, and the castle walls. Climbing to the top of the Tower of Lions provides wonderful views of the remains of the fortress. You can look out over the gardens, or look down to the castle wall below. At the other end of the wall is the famous Inquisition tower, which was used as a prison during the Spanish Inquisition. The Alcázar was the headquarters of the Inquisition in 1482. Visitors can enter one of the tower rooms to see the high, narrow window slits, and the bolts that held chains in the wall. Boabdil, the last Moorish King of Granada, was a prisoner here. When he refused to surrender the city of Granada, Ferdinand and Isabel attacked it, and successfully conquered the city in 1492.

If that date sounds familiar to Americans, it's because 1492 is when Columbus discovered the Americas. He had spent several years petitioning the monarchs of various European courts, but no one was willing to finance his quest. After King Ferdinand and Queen Isabella defeated the Moors at Granada in 1492, they were flush with war winnings and low on enemies, so they met with Columbus at Córdoba's Alcázar to commission him for his first voyage. A statue in the palace gardens commemorates that event.

Entrance fee is 8 Euros for adults. The Alcázar is open from 10 am- 3 pm, and again from 5- 7 pm. Admission is FREE on Wednesdays. Bring some water, because the gardens can get quite sunny, and Cordoba in general is hot in the spring and summer months.

Final note about Córdoba: the city is famous for its Festival of the Patios, which occurs every May. You can enter private patios and see the amazing blooms and tile decorations. Some offer refreshments or have musical entertainment, because they compete for a prestigious prize from the city. Pick up a map from the Tourist Office to see which patios are participating. At any time of year, there are numerous patio-style restaurants in the area around the Mezquita and the Alcázar where tourists can enjoy shade, refreshments, and typical Córdoban flowers and decor.

GRANADA

Granada is a large, sprawling city with a modern urban vibe. If you are used to visiting quaint, dusty, mountain villages in Spain, you will be surprised by Granada's metropolitan center, shining store windows, and international cuisine. There are great reasons to visit Granada throughout the year. In warm weather, tourists flock to the Alhambra—the last Moorish stronghold, and most richly decorated palace. In winter, the mountains around Granada are snow-covered. This is one of the only sources of snow within driving distance of Rota, so if your children have lived in Spain too long and don't know how to build a snowman, consider spending a winter weekend here. The sledding and skiing opportunities are in the Sierra Nevada mountains around the city, about 20-30 minutes away. Do research ahead of time, because some slopes have restrictions on equipment or ages of children.

The main attraction in Granada is the Alhambra. This is a huge palace complex, high on the hill overlooking the city. It was the last stronghold of the Moorish kings, and is a stunning example of *mudejar* architecture: extremely intricate carvings on walls and window lattices, pointed archways, elaborate fountains, and gorgeous gardens. The fortress was mostly constructed in the 11th century, replacing a small 8th century fort. It became a palace in the 13th century, with each Muslim ruler adding to it and improving it. Later, the Christian kings conquered Granada and used the Alhambra for themselves. In the 16th century Charles V added his own palace to the grounds. So the complex now contains several structures and gardens from different time periods, all included with your ticket purchase.

The fanciest building, the Nasrid Palace, is the star of the show and the area most people come to see. It has the famous Court of Lions and the Hall of the Abencerrajes with its 'honeycomb' ceiling. You should order tickets months in advance, because the number of visitors allowed in the Nasrid Palace is limited. Tickets sell out quickly, especially in the summer months. You can visit either in the morning or in the afternoon. When you order online, you can either take your email confirmation to the main ticket entrance of the Alhambra to pick up your tickets, or you can bring your confirmation email ahead of time to any Caixa bank to get your tickets. If you have actual tickets in hand, you can use a side entrance to the complex that is a little closer and more convenient, and you don't have to wait in the regular ticket line.

**Tickets for the Alhambra should be purchased in advance.
Visit: http://www.alhambradegranada.org/en/
to make a reservation.**

A specific time will be printed on your e-mail and ticket. This is your time to enter the Nasrid Palace, near the far end of the complex. You can enter the Alhambra area before your ticket time and visit the gardens, the fort, and the Palace of Charles V. But you cannot enter the Nasrid Palace without lining up at your appropriate time. I recommend arriving at the Alhambra at least 1 hour before your ticket time, because it takes at least 30 minutes to walk from the main entrance area, across the gardens, to the area where the Nasrid Palace line forms. Do not miss your ticket time, because then you won't be allowed in! It takes about 1 hour to explore the rooms of the palace, and it is an experience you will remember for a long time. Each room is more exotic and impressive than the next.

If possible, spend a full day exploring the rest of the grounds. They are mostly stroller accessible, but there is a stroller check. The rest of the Alhambra includes the walls and tower of the Alcazaba fort (the oldest building there) which you can climb via many stairs; the Renaissance-style palace of Charles V, with a round columned courtyard; and the palace and gardens of the Generalife (pronounced Hen-er-al-leaf-ay). This Moorish style palace is not as elaborate as the Nasrid Palace, but it has amazing gardens and fountains. Washington Irving, the American writer, lived in the Alhambra in 1828. He wrote about his experiences, including local tales and legends. Read his book *Tales of the Alhambra* before you go, to enrich your visit.

Other Granada sites include the neo-classical Cathedral and surrounding spice markets. King Ferdinand and Queen Isabella are buried in the cathedral. Some visitors enjoy hiking uphill through the very narrow, steep streets of the Albaycin, the old Moorish area of the city. In Sacromonte are the cave-homes of gypsies, where you can see wonderful dance shows with vibrant flamenco music. Finally, Granada is one of the few cities in Spain that still serves free tapas. These are complimentary whenever drinks are ordered at a bar.

LISBON, PORTUGAL

Lisboa, the capital of Portugal, is a 5-hour drive from Rota, and definitely worth visiting. It has a great variety of medieval charm, rich museums, beautiful architecture, and modern shopping, dining, and nightlife. There is something for everyone, whether you are looking for a romantic escape to fairy-tale castles, or a fun trip with children. Yes, they speak Portuguese, which looks similar to Spanish but has a completely unique sound. However, English is widely spoken in all tourist areas, so we had no trouble getting around.

The drive to Lisbon will take you through the rural part of Southern Portugal, where fields of olive trees, sheep, and cows dominate the landscape. The tolls on the route are very steep. You present your credit card at a kiosk when you cross the border, and then small fees are automatically charged every few miles. In 2014, a Category 1 (small car) paid about 20 Euros in tolls each way. But a minivan is Category 2 and pays twice as much. So remember to plan tolls, gas, and parking expenses into your vacation budget. Also, note that Lisbon's time zone is 1 hour ahead of Madrid's.

Lisbon is built on seven hills, each with its own personality. Research to find lodging on the one that suits you. For example, one has loud nightlife, one has great shopping, and another has a medieval castle. Try to limit your walking tours, because it is a VERY hilly city, with steep staircases that climb several stories at a time just to reach the next block. Children will tire quickly, and it is NOT stroller friendly, so consider using a baby backpack instead.

ST. GEORGE'S CASTLE: Perched high on the Alfama hill, this castle is a well-preserved medieval masterpiece. Children can play on the ramparts for free, or you can pay the entrance fee to tour the castle and visit the small archaeological museum inside. Either way, the views are gorgeous and worth the climb!

CATHEDRAL: The city's largest cathedral, called the Sé, is a Romanesque building with arching stone ceilings, stained glass rosette windows, and huge paintings.

YELLOW TROLLEY CARS: these iconic, old-fashioned cars are the public transportation on the streets of Lisbon (there is a metro underground). They are especially popular in the old part of town, around the cathedral, where you can board certain lines and pay a minimal fee for a scenic ride.

AQUARIUM: One of the best aquariums around, the Oceanarium in Lisbon is a huge cube structure with enormous tanks on each side, representing the different oceans and their ecosystems. It can be reached by metro, and is located at the edge of the city.

CHRIST STATUE: The enormous statue of Christ overlooks the city from across the river. It was built in 1959 in thanksgiving for surviving WWII, and is modeled after the statue in Rio de Janeiro. You can reach it by ferry, then take a bus ride to the statue and an elevator several hundred feet to the top. Incredible views!

BRIDGE: The enormous suspension bridge that crosses the Tagus River is called the 25 de Avril, after Lisbon's revolution. Americans will be reminded of the Golden Gate bridge in San Francisco, which it is modeled after. Lisbon's bridge currently has the longest central span in Europe.

ART AND ARCHITECTURE: Whether you visit an art museum, the beautiful Belem tower, or the Jeronimos monastery, there is plenty of colorful culture to experience.

SINTRA: a city just outside Lisbon which is considered "the essential day trip" from the city, because of its high concentration of gorgeous castles and mansions. It was the summer retreat area for Lisbon's royalty. The most famous is the Pena Palace, with high turrets, beautiful domes, and bright pastel colors. You can drive 40 minutes from the city, or take a metro ride lasting about 30 minutes.

FATIMA: a Catholic pilgrimage site about 1 hour north of Lisbon. This is where the Blessed Mother appeared to three children six times in 1917, and demonstrated the miracle of the sun. A huge church is now built on the site of the apparitions, where Mass and Confessions are regularly available in multiple languages.

MADRID

Spain's capital in centrally-located, about 6-7 hours driving from Rota. The only major highway toll is the one near Sevilla. Madrid can also be reached by train in 4 hours, or by plane from Jerez airport in 45 minutes. There are so many reasons to visit Spain's most important city!

PLAZA MAYOR: This is the central square of Spain's historic district. Flanked by 16th century buildings and containing a huge statue of Phillip III (as well as the Tourism Office), it is a must-see for visitors. Excellent shopping can be found in the nearby streets, or in the flagship store of El Corte Ingles nearby. On New Years' Eve, all of Spain listens to the bells chime in this square, and races to swallow one grape on each chime.

ART MUSEUMS: The Prado is internationally-renowned, and an amazing collection of Western Art. Of course it is the world's best collection of Spanish art, with pieces from all the masters. But it also has great examples of Italian and French Renaissance art. Plan to spend at least half a day here. There are also other art museums in the city, dedicated to other periods and styles.

PALACE: The gorgeous white royal residence was built in the 1700's with all the splendor of that century. The exterior is similar to the Louvre in Paris, but the interior is full of gold, and reminiscent of the castle of Versailles. Since it is no longer used by the royal family, the entire palace is a museum. Admission fees are usually 10 Euros (2014), but FREE entrance times are available for EU citizens each afternoon—just show your Spanish driver's license.

CULTURAL ACTIVITIES: Madrid is the ideal location to watch a fútbol match (at Bernabéu Stadium), witness a bullfight (Las Ventas is the largest bullring in Spain), or see a flamenco show while enjoying tapas or dinner (performances are available nightly at cafés and bars throughout Madrid.)

PARKS AND BEACH: Even though Madrid is landlocked, it still has a unique city beach, complete with sand and pools of water. The River Park, or Parque Rio, is a new green area that stretches 10 km along the Manzanares River at the western and southern edges of Madrid. A major highway used to run along the river, but when the road was moved underground, the area was redeveloped into a beautiful public park with playgrounds, jogging paths, great scenery, and a sandy beach. Other green areas include the El Retiro Park with gorgeous fountains and the Crystal Palace, or the Botanical Gardens, which contain 20 acres of plants. There is a small entrance fee for the Botanical Gardens.

MARATHON: Every year, Madrid hosts the Rock and Roll marathon and half marathon, which has a course leading past some of the city's most important sights. Runners can also participate in shorter distances. MWR usually coordinates a trip for anyone wanting to participate in this event.

TOLEDO

medieval city of Toledo, once the capital of Spain, is located in the center of the country, about an hour southwest of Madrid. It is a gorgeous city. Most people see Toledo as a day trip from Madrid, and there are numerous trains and busses that run between Toledo and the capital every day. Consider spending a weekend relaxing in one place and enjoying the quiet, slow-paced city. Other nearby day trips include the medieval towns of Segovia and Avila—each about an hour from Toledo. From Rota, Toledo is a straightforward 5 hour drive, and the only toll is the one near Sevilla.

Toledo is famous for several reasons. First, the city is surrounded on three sides by the Tagus River, so it has not expanded or changed much since the Middle Ages. The streets are still ridiculously narrow, designed for pedestrians long before motorized traffic. Therefore, it is NOT advised to drive in Toledo. Get very clear directions to your hotel, verify that there is parking somewhere, and then don't plan to use your car again until you leave. The upsides to this are that the city is very quiet, and still maintains Medieval charm. Besides, you can cover the whole city easily on foot, so there is no need for taxis.

Toledo is called the "city of three cultures," because Jews, Christians, and Moors were allowed to thrive and influence each other. While the Jews and Muslims were eventually driven out of Toledo by a Christian majority, it was not a destructive removal, and the cultural respect remained. So you can see numerous Moorish *mudejar* style buildings, and their architectural influence is more evident than in most cities in Southern Spain.

The most famous building is the Alcázar castle, which has been a stronghold for thousands of years—for the Romans in the 3rd century, the Moors in the 1000's, the Christian Kings in the 1500's— and it even withheld a siege of Republicans during the Spanish Civil War in the 1940's. It was mostly destroyed after that. It has been rebuilt and is now an army museum. It dominates the skyline, just as it was painted by El Greco in the late 1500's.

El Greco, the painter, is one of the city's most famous inhabitants. The title means "The Greek," and was the nickname of Domenikos Theotokopoulos, who moved to Toledo toward the end of his career, in 1577. Although he struggled to gain approval from the Spanish court, he is now universally renowned for his use of light and color and for his elongated human figures. Toledo is quite proud of him, and has several places where you can view his work. His famous painting "The Burial of Count Orgaz" is an enormous work covering a whole wall in the church of Santo Tome. There is also the Museo El Greco, a recently restored and reopened museum on the Western edge of the city. The museum has been built to imitate his house and demonstrate a wealthy household in the 1500's. Entrance fees are 5 Euros per adult, kids free (2014). There are not a lot of works here, since his paintings have been scattered throughout the world. There is one long gallery with all Greco's original paintings of Christ and the Apostles, some of his best portraits.

One of our favorite activities in the city was going on the "train" ride. This is actually a trolley, shaped like a train, that drives on city streets and takes you across the river to see every side of the city. It makes a big circle from the Plaza Zocodover, and the trip lasts just under 1 hour. Their website is Toledo Train Vision: www.busvision.net. Adult fees were 6 Euros, 3 Euros for kids, (younger kids free). Sit on the right side of the bench to get the best pictures. You will drive around the Alcázar, then past the main gate and out of the city, enjoying beautiful views and listening to interesting history on the headphones.

Toledo's Cathedral is an amazing structure that took over 200 years to build—from the 1200's to the 1500's, which was Toledo's Golden Age. You will see every style of Renaissance art inside: Gothic, High Gothic, and Baroque. It is one of the most impressive Gothic cathedrals in Spain. Tickets are 6 Euros per adult (kids free), and can be purchased in the shop directly across from the tour entrance, on the Southern side of the church. The stained glass windows are gorgeous. There are more than 700 in the Cathedral, and their colors are phenomenal! The best time to visit the Cathedral is in the morning, when the sunlight shines through the *Transparente*. This is a unique Baroque element in the Cathedral. In the 1500's, a huge hole was cut into the ceiling to allow more light to shine on the back of the altarpiece. The area around the *transparente* is decorated with painted Baroque saints and angels, as well as carved 3-D figures surrounding the hole, making it look like a window to heaven. A small hole is also present in the altarpiece, so in the morning the sun lights up the tabernacle from behind. The golden *retable*, or elaborate wall of paintings behind the altar, stretches from floor to ceiling, and shows important scenes from Jesus's life painted in bright colors on gold and silver backgrounds. It is truly gorgeous and breathtaking.

The Cathedral has a number of other additional interesting sights. In the Treasury you can see an enormous monstrance, over 10 feet tall, made from 18 kilos of gold and 183 kilos of silver! It is used in the city's Corpus Christi procession, in early June, which is their largest annual festival. The streets are decorated weeks in advance, and the monstrance is processed carrying the Body of Christ. The Treasury is located in one corner of the Cathedral, and admission is included with your general tour ticket. The Chapterhouse, or *Salla Capitular*, is a room designed and built around 1500, which serves as the meeting place for Spain's bishops. Although Toledo ceased to be the political capital of the country when the kings moved to Madrid in the 1600's, Toledo is still the religious center of Spain. On all four walls are portraits of the Archbishops of Toledo, from the present all the way back to Saint Eugene in 300 A.D.

Toledo is a perfect city for window shopping. The two specialty products of Toledo are swords and *damasque* (the unique art of inlaying gold on burnished silver), and both can be viewed in almost every shop in every area of the city. The city was a center of sword-making since Roman times, when the weapons for the Punic Wars were forged here. *Damasque* was an Islamic art form that used gold provided by the Jewish community and images and scenes provided by the Christian community. You can purchase *damasque* jewelry, plates, and small decorative objects. Another fun thing to shop for in Toledo is pastries and *marzipan*. Marzipan is a sweet paste made from almonds and honey, which can be formed into almost any shape or design. The legend is that it was created by nuns during one of Toledo's many famines. They did not have any flour, so they ground up almonds (which grow plentifully in this region) and mixed them with honey to create a substance that was nourishing and supposedly saved the city. A *Toledana* is a pastry roll filled with thick almond jelly.

In summary, Toledo is an amazing, gorgeous, enjoyable city, with tons of Medieval charm, and lots to entertain lovers of art, history, or shopping. I hope you will get a chance to enjoy it!

TRAVEL NOTES:

ABOUT THE AUTHOR

Lizann Lightfoot has had the honor of being a military spouse for the past seven years, and now has four young children with her Marine Corps husband. Rota was their third duty station together. They have enjoyed exploring Spain, and look forward to new adventures in the future.

Lizann was an English major in college, and has always been interested in writing and publishing. This is her first book. Photos, recipes, and more travel information about Spain can be found on her blog:
www.adventuresinrota.blogspot.com.

SLO - www.navymwrrota.com/program

/18fe4fcd-189f-4539-9a59-
59663922fbb8.

Reg - smore.com/rgemr

Rota DFG Middle School

SLORota@eu.navy.mil

Pets - Rota-Vet-Clinic/
1778 7634556/231 ?
fref=ts

Made in the USA
Coppell, TX
25 April 2023

16018258R00118